THE LITURGY

OF

JOHN KNOX

THE LITURGY

OF

JOHN KNOX

Received by the Church of Scotland in 1564

WIPF & STOCK · Eugene, Oregon

Wipf and Stock Publishers
199 W 8th Ave, Suite 3
Eugene, OR 97401

The Liturgy of John Knox
By Knox, John
ISBN 13: 978-1-60608-305-5
Publication date 01/08/2009
Previously published by Glasgow University Press, 1886

Editorial Note.

THERE are few Scotchmen who, being impressed with a sense of regard for the religious history of their country, can fail to look with considerable interest on the series of Confessions, Orders, and Forms which commonly go under the designation of *John Knox's Liturgy*, but more officially termed the *Book of Common Order*, printed in part before 1564, and formally adopted by the Assembly of the Church of Scotland in that year. These formularies were in more or less general use down to the time of the Solemn League and Covenant, when they were superseded by the Confession, Catechism, and Directions, prepared by the Westminster Assembly. Numerous editions of *Knox's Liturgy* continued to be printed, chiefly at Edinburgh and Aberdeen, till 1643. All of which though, strange to say, are exceeding scarce, and a complete copy of any of the editions very rarely to be met with.

In more recent times, three editions have been

issued—one of these in 1831, edited by the Rev. Edward Irving; another in 1840, edited by the Rev. Dr. Cumming, of London; and a third in 1868, edited by the Rev. George W. Sprott and the Rev. Thomas Leishman. These issues, now all exceedingly scarce also, have (unfortunately, as some would think) been modernized in matters of spelling and other features, thus taking from the book much of that quaintness which in the estimation of many ought to be an inherent feature in the work. In the present issue the old spelling and phraseology, as in the 1565 edition, is strictly adhered to, and it likewise contains all that characterizes the best of the older editions.

When in use, the Liturgy was commonly issued along with the Psalms, but in other instances the Liturgy and Psalms were issued separately. This early translation of the Psalms is peculiarly quaint, interesting, and expressive, and differs widely from the more modern one. It was in use down to 1650, when the somewhat recent translation was adopted. This early version will, it is intended, be issued shortly, as a companion volume to, and uniform with, the present one.

The Liturgy

of

John Knox

THE LITURGY

OF

JOHN KNOX.

The Confession of Faith

Used in the Englishe Congregation at Geneva.

Received and Approved by the Church of Scotland.

I BELEVE and confesse my Lorde God eternal, infinite, unmeasurable, incomprehensible, and invisible, one in substance, and three in persone, Father, Sonne, and Holy Ghoste, who, by his almightie power and wisdome, hathe not onely of nothinge created heaven, earthe, and all thinges therein conteyned, and man after his owne image, that he might in hym be glorifiede; but also by his fatherlye providence, governeth, maynteyneth, and preserveth the same, according to the purpose of his will.

I beleve also and confesse Jesus Christe the onely Saviour and Messias, who beinge equall with God, made him self of no reputation, but tooke on him the shape of a servant, and became man in all thinges like unto us (synne except) to assure us of mercie and forgivenes. For when through our father Adam's transgression we were become childrene of perdition, there was no meanes to bring us from that yoke of synne and damnation, but onely Jesus Christe our Lord: who givinge us that by grace, which was his by nature, made us (through faith) the childrene of God: who when the fulnes of tyme was come, was conceyved by the power of the Holy Ghoste, borne of the Virgine Marie (accordinge to the fleshe), and at lenght, by tyrannye of the priestes, he was gilteles condemned under Pontius Pilate, then president of Jurie, and most slaunderously hanged on the crosse betwixte two theves as a notorious trespasser, where takinge upon hym the punishement of our synnes, he delyvered us frome the curse of the Lawe.

And forasmoche as he, beinge onely God, could not feele deathe, nether, beinge onely man, could overcome deathe, he joined bothe together, and suffred his humanitie to be punished with moste cruell death: felinge in him selfe the anger and severe judgement of God, even as if he had bene in the extreme tormentes of hell, and therfore cryed with a lowde voice, "My God, my God, why haste thou forsaken me?" Thus of his fre mercie, without compulsion, he offred up him selfe as the onely sacrifice to purge the synnes of all the world, so that all other sacrifices for synne are blasphemous and derogate from the sufficiencie herof. The which death, albeit it did sufficiently reconcile us to God; yet the Scriptures commonly do attribute our regeneration to hys resurrection; for as by rysinge agayn frome the grave the third day, he conquered death; evenso the victorie of our faith standeth in his resurrection, and therfore without the one, we can not fele the benefite of the other: For as by deathe, synne was taken awaye, so our rightuousnes was restored by his resurrection.

And because he wolde accomplishe all thinges, and take possession for us in his kingdome, he ascended into heaven, to enlarge that same kingdome by the aboundant power of his Spirite, by whome we are moste assured of his contynuall intercession towardes God the Father for us. And althoghe he be in heaven, as towchinge his corporall presence, where the Father hathe nowe set him on his right hand, committinge unto him the administration of all things, aswel in heaven above as in the earthe benethe; yet is he present with us his membres, even to the ende of the world, in preservinge and goverynge us with his effectuall power and grace, who (when all thinges are fulfilled which God hath spoken by the mowth of all hys prophets since the world began) wyll come in the same visible forme in the which he ascended, with an unspekable majestie, power, and companye, to separate the lambes frome the goates, th'electe from the reprobate, so that none, whether he be alyve then or deade before, shall escape his judgement.

MOREOVER, I beleve and confesse the Holy Ghoste, God equall with the Father and the Sonne, whoe regenerateth and sanctifieth us, ruleth and guideth us into all trueth, persuadinge moste assuredly in our consciences that we be the childrene of God, bretherne to Jesus Christe, and fellowe heires with him of lyfe everlastinge. Yet notwithstandinge it is not sufficient to beleve that God is omnipotent and mercifull; that Christ hath made satisfaction; or, that the Holye Ghoste hath this power and effect, except we do applie the same benefites to our selves which are God's elect.

I BELIEVE therfore and confesse one holye Churche, which (as members of Jesus Christe, th'onely heade therof) consent in faithe, hope, and charitie, usinge the giftes of God, whether they be temporall or spirituall, to the profite and furtherance of the same. Whiche Churche is not sene to man's eye, but onely knowen to God, who of the loste sonnes of Adam, hath ordeyned some, as vessels of wrathe, to damnation, and hathe chosen others, as vessels of his mercie, to be saved; the whiche also, in due tyme, he callethe to integritie of lyfe and godly conversation, to make them a glorious church to him selfe.

But that Churche which is visible, and sene to the eye, hathe three tokens, or markes, wherby it may be discerned. First, the Worde of God conteyned in the Olde and Newe Testament, which as it is above the autoritie of the same churche, and onely sufficient to instruct us in all

OF FAITH.

thinges concernynge salvation, so is it left for all degrees of men to reade and understand. For without this Worde, neither churche, concile, or decree can establishe any point touching salvation.

The second is the holy Sacraments, to witt, of Baptisme and the Lordes Supper; which Sacramentes Christ hathe left unto us as holie signes and seales of God's promesses. For as by Baptisme once receyved, is signified that we (aswel infants as others of age and discretion) being straungers from God by originall synne, are receyved into his familie and congregation, with full assurance, that althoghe this roote of synne lye hyd in us, yet to the electe it shal not be imputed. So the Supper declareth, that God, as a most provident Father, doth not onely fede our bodies, but also spiritually nourisheth our soules with the graces and benefites of Jesus Christ (which the Scripture calleth eatinge of his flesh and drinkinge of his bloode); nether must we, in the administration of these sacraments, followe man's phantasie, but as Christ him self hath ordeyned so must they be ministred, and by suche as by ordinarie vocation are therunto called. Therfor, whosoever reserveth and worshippeth these sacraments, or contrariwyse contemneth them in tyme and place, procureth to him self damnation.

The third marke of this Church is Ecclesiasticall discipline, which standeth in admonition and correction of fautes. The finall ende wherof is excommunication, by the consent of the Churche determyned, if the offender be obstinate. And besides this Ecclesiasticall censure, I acknowlage to belonge to this church a politicall Magistrate, who ministreth to every man justice, defending the good and punishinge the evell; to whom we must rendre honor and obedience in all thinges, which are not contrarie to the Word of God.

And as Moses, Ezechias, Josias, and other godly rulers purged the Church of God frome superstition and idolatrie, so the defence of Christes Church apperteynith to the Christian Magistrates, against all idolaters and heretikes, as Papistes, Anabaptistes, with such like limmes of Antechrist, to roote owte all doctrine of devels and men, as the Masse, Purgatorie, *Limbus Patrum*, prayer to Sanctes, and for the Deade; freewyll, distinction of meates, apparell, and days; vows of single life, presence at idoll service, man's merites, with suchlike, which drawe us frome the societie of Christes Churche, wherein standeth onely remission of synnes, purchased by Christes bloode to all them that beleve, whether they be Jewes or Gentiles, and leade us to vayne confidence in creatures, and trust in our owne imaginations. The punishement wherof, althogh God often tymes differreth in this lyfe, yet after the generall resurrection, when our sowles and bodies shall ryse agayne to immortalitie, they shalbe damned to inquencheable fyer; and then we which have forsaken all man's wisdome to cleave unto Christ, shall heare that joyfull voice, "Come, ye blessed of my Father, inherite ye the kingdome prepared for you frome the beginnyng of the world," and so shall go triumphing with him in bodye and soule, to remayne everlasting in glorie, where we shall see God face to face, and shall no more nede one to instructe an other; for we shall all knowe him, from the hyghest to the loweste: To whome, withe the Sonne and the Holy Ghost, be all praise, honor, and glorie, nowe and ever. So be it.

Of the Ministers and their Election.

What thinges are chiefely required in the Ministers.

FIRST, let the Churche diligently consider that the Minister which is to be chosen be not founde culpable of any suche fautes which Saincte Paul reprehendeth in a man of that vocation, but contrarywise endewed with suche vertues, that he may be able to undertake his charge, and diligently execute the same. Secondly, that he distribute faithfully the Word of God, and minister the sacraments sincerely, ever carefull not onely to teache his flock publikly, but also privatly to admonisshe them; remembring alwais, that if any thinge perysshe throughe his defaute, the Lorde will require it at his handes.

Of their Office and Deutie.

BECAWSE the charge of the Word of God is of greater importaunce then that any man is able to dispence therwith; and Saincte Paule exhorteth to esteme them as ministers of Christe, and disposers of God's mysteries; not lordes or rulers, as S. Peter saith over the flocke. Therfore the pastor's or minister's chief office standeth in preaching the Worde of God, and ministring the sacraments. So that in consultations, judgementes, elections, and other politicall affairs, his counsel, rather then autoritie, taketh place.

OF THE MINISTERS.

And if so be the Congregation, uppon juste cawse, agreeth to excommunicate, then it belongeth to the minister, according to their general determination, to pronounce the sentence, to the end that all thinges may be done orderly, and withoute confusion.

The manner of Electinge the Ministers.

THE Ministers and Elders at suche time as there wanteth a Minister, assemble the whole Congregation, exhortinge them to advise and consider who may best serve in that rowme and office. And if there be choyse, the Churche appoynte two or thre, upon sume certayne day, to be examined by the Ministers and Elders.

First, as towchyng their doctrine, whether he that should be minister have good and sownde knowlage in the Holy Scriptures, and fitte and apte giftes to communicate the same to the edification of the people. For the triall wherof, they propose hym a theme or text to be treated privatly, wherby his habilitie may the more manifestlie appeare unto them.

Secondly, they enquire of his life and conversation, if he have in times past lyved without slander, and governed hym selfe in suche sorte, as the Worde of God hath not hearde evel, or bene slandered through his occasion. Which being severallie done, they signifie unto the Congregation, whose giftes they fynde moste excellent and profitable for that ministerie. Appoynting by a generall consent, eight daies at the leaste, that every man may diligently inquire of his life and manners.

At the which tyme also, the minister exhorteth them to humble them selves to God by fasting and prayer, that bothe their election may be agreable to his will, and also profitable to the Churche. And if in the meane season any thyng be brought agaynst hym wherby he may be fownde unworthy by lawfull probations, then is he dismissed and some other presented. If nothing be alleaged uppon some certayne day, one of the ministers, at the mornyng sermon, presenteth hym agayne to the Churche, framyng his sermon, or some parte therof, to the settyng forthe of his dewtie.

Then at after none, the sermon ended, the minister exhortith them to the election, with the invocation of God's name, directing his prayer as God shal move his herte. In like manner, after the election, the Minister geveth thankes to God, with request of suche thinges as shalbe necessarie for his office.

After that he is appointed Minister, the people syng a psalme and departe.

Of the Elders, and as touchyng their Office and Election.

THE Elders must be men of good lyfe and godly conversation, withoute blame and all suspition;

carefull for the flocke, wise, and, above all thynges, fearing God. Whose office standeth in gouverning with the rest of the ministers, in consulting, admonisshing, correcting, and ordering all thynges appertayning to the state of the congregation. And they differ from the ministers, in that they preache not the Worde, nor minister the Sacramentes. In assemblyng the people, nether they withoute the ministers, nor the ministers withoute them, may attempt any thing. And if any of the juste nombre want, the minister, by the consent of the rest, warneth the people thereof, and finalye admonissheth them to observe the same ordre which was used in chosing the Ministers.

Of the Deacons, and their Office and Election.

THE Deacons must be men of good estimation and report, discret, of good conscience; charitable, wyse, and finallye adorned with suche vertues as S. Paul requireth in them. Their office is to gather the aulmes diligentlie, and faithfullie to distribute it, with the consent of the Ministers and Elders. Also to provyde for the sicke and impotent personnes. Having ever a diligent care, that the charitie of godlye men be not wasted upon loytrers and ydle vagabondes. Their election is, as hath bene afore rehearsed in the Ministers and Elders.

OF THE TEACHERS.

We are not ignorante that the Scriptures make mention of a fourthe kynde of Ministers left to the Churche of Christe, which also are very profitable, where tyme and place dothe permit. But for lacke of opportunitie, in this oure dispersion and exile, we can not well have the use therof; and wolde to God it were not neglected where better occasion serveth.

These Ministers are called Teachers or Doctors, whose office is to instructe and teache the faithfull in sownde doctrine, providing with all diligence that the puritie of the Gospell be not corrupt, either through ignorance, or evill opinions. Notwithstandyng, considering the present state of thynges, we comprehend under this title suche meanes as God hathe in his Churche, that it shuld not be left desolate, nor yet his doctrine decaye for defaut of ministers therof.

Therfore to terme it by a worde more usuall in these our days, we may call it th'Order of Schooles, wherin the highest degree, and moste annexed to the ministerie and governement of the Churche, is the exposition of Godes Worde, which is contayned in the Olde and Newe Testamentes.

But becawse menne cannot so well proffet in that knowledge, except they be first instructed in the tonges and humaine sciences, (for now God worketh not commonlie by miracles,) it is necessarie that seed be sowen for the tyme to come, to the intent that the Churche be not left

*barren and waste to our posteritie; and that
Scholes also be erected, and Colledges mayn-
tayned, with juste and sufficient stipendes,
wherin youthe may be trayned in the knowledge and feare of God, that in their ripe age
they may prove worthy members of our Lorde
Jesus Christ, whether it be to rule in Civill
policie, or to serve in the Spirituall ministerie,
or els to lyve in godly reverence and subjection.*

The Weekly Assemblie of the Ministers, Elders, and Deacons.

To the intent that the ministerie of Godes
Woorde may be had in reverence, and not
brought to contempt through the evill conversation of suche as are called therunto, and also
that fautes and vices may not by long sufferance
growe at length to extreme inconveniences; it is
ordeyned that every Thursdaye the ministers and
elders, in their assemblie or Consistorie, diligentlie
examine all suche fautes and suspicions as may be
espied, not onelie amongest others, but chieflie
amongest theym selves, lest they seme to be
culpable of that which our Saviour Christ
reproved in the Pharisies, who coulde espie
a mote in an other man's eye, and could not see
a beame in their owne.

And becawse the eye ought to be more cleare
then the rest of the bodie, the minister may not
be spotted with any vice, but to the great
slaunder of Godes Woorde, whose message he

beareth: Therfore it is to be understand that there be certayne fautes, which if they be deprehended in a minister, he oght to be deposed; as heresie, papistrie, schisme, blasphemie, perjurie, fornication, thefte, dronkennes, usurie, fighting, unlawfull games, with suche like.

Others are more tollerable, if so be that after brotherlie admonition he amendith his faut: as strange and unprofitable fashon in preaching the Scriptures; curiositie in sekyng vayne questions; negligence, aswell in his sermons, and in studying the Scriptures, as in all other thynges concerning his vocation; scurrilitie, flattering, lying, backbyting, wanton woordes, deceipt, covetousnes, tauntyng, dissolution in apparell, gesture, and other his doynges; which vices, as they be odious in all men, so in hym that ought to be as an example to others of perfection, in no wise are to be suffred; especially, if so be that, according to Godes rule, being brotherlie advertised, he acknowledge not his faut and amend.

Interpretation of the Scriptures.

EVERIE weeke once, the Congregation assemble to heare some place of the Scriptures orderly expounded. At which tyme, it is lawfull for every man to speake or enquire, as God shall move his harte, and the text minister occasion; so it be without pertinacitee or disdayne, as one that rather seketh to proffit then to contend. And if so be any contencion rise, then suche as are

THE WEEKLY ASSEMBLY. 23

appointed moderatours, either satisfie the partie, or els if he seme to cavill, exhorte hym to kepe silence, referring the judgement therof to the ministers and elders, to be determined in their assemblie or Consistorie before mencioned.

The Forme and Ordour

of the

Electioun of the Superintendents,

Quhilk may serve also in Electioun of all uther Ministers.

At Edinburghe the 9th of Merche 1560 yeiris, Johne Knox being Minister.

First was made a Sermone, in the quhilk thir Heids war intreated. First, The necessity of Ministers and Superintendents. 2. The crymes and vyces that micht unable thame [of the ministrie]. 3. The vertues required in thame. And last, Quhidder sick as by publict consent of the Kyrk wer callit to sick Office, micht refuis the same.

The Sermone finisched, it was declared be the same Minister, (maker thareof,) that the Lords of Secrete Councell had given charge and power to the Kirkis of Lauthiane, to chuse Mr. Johne Spottiswode Superintendent; and that sufficient warning was made be publict edict to the Kirks of Edinburghe, Linlythgow, Striveling, Tranent, Hadingtoun, and Dunbar; as also to Earles, Lords, Barones, Gentilmen, and uthers, having, or quho micht clame to have voite in Electioun, to be present that day, at that same hour: And, therefore, inquisitioun was made, Quho wer present, and quho wer absent.

Efter was called the said **Mr.** Johne, quho answering; the Minister demanded, Gif ony man knew ony cryme or offence to the said Mr. Johne, that mycht unabill him to be called to that office? And this he demanded thryis. Secundlie, Questioun was moved to the haill multitude, If thair was ony uther quhome they wald put in Electioun with the said Mr. Johne. The pepill wer asked, If they wald have the said Mr. Johne Superintendent? If they wald honour and obey him as Christis Minister? and comfort and assist him in every thing perteining to his Charge?

They Answerit.

We will; and we do promeis unto him sick obedience as becumethe the scheip to give unto thair Pastour, sa lang as he remains faythfull in his office.

The Answers of the Pepill, and thair consents receaved, thir Questiouns wer proponit unto him that was to be elected.

Questioun.—Seing that ye hear the thrist and desyre of this people, do ye not think yourself bound in conscience befoir God to support thame that so earnestly call for your comfort, and for the fruit of your labours?

Answer.—If anie thing wer in me abill to satisfie thair desyir, I acknowledge myself bound to obey God calling by thame.

Questioun.—Do ye seik to be promoted to this Office and charge, for ony respect of warldly commoditie, riches or glory?

Answer.—God knawes the contrarie.

Questioun.—Beleve ye not that the doctrine of the Propheits and Apostles, conteined in the buiks of the Auld and New Testaments, is the onely trew and most absolute foundatioun of the universall Kirk of Christ Jesus, insamekill that in the same Scriptures ar conteined all things necessary to be beleved for the salvatioun of Mankind?

Answer.—I verely beleve the same, and do abhorre and utterly refuis all Doctrine alleged necessary to Salvatioun, that is not expressedly conteined in the same.

Questioun.—Is not Christ Jesus Man of Man, according to the flesche, to wit, the Sone of David, the Seid of Abrahame, conceaved by the Holy Ghost, borne of the Virgin Marie his mother, the onely Head and Mediatour of his Kirk?

Answer.—He is, and without him thair is nouther salvatioun to man, nor lyfe to angell.

Questioun.—Is not the same Lord Jesus, [the] onely trew God, the Eternall Sone of the Eternall Father, in quhome all that sall be saved wer elected befoir the foundatioun of the world was layd?

Answer.—I confes and acknawlege him in the unitie of his Godheid, to be God above all thingis, blessit for evir.

Questioun.—Sall not they quhome God in his eternall councell hes electit, be callit to the knawlege of his Sone, our Lord Jesus? And sall not they, quho of purpoise are elected in this lyfe, be justified? And is not justificatioun and free remissioun of sinnes obtained in this lyfe by free grace? Sall not this glorie of the sonnes of God follow in the generall resurrectioun, quhen the Sone of God sall appeir in his glorious majesty?

Answer.—I acknawlege this to be the doctrine of the Apostles, and the most singular comfort of God's childrein.

Questioun.—Will ye not contein yourself in all doctrine within the boundes of this foundatioun? Will ye not study to promote the same, alsweill by your lyfe as by your doctrine? Will ye not, according to the graces and utterance that God sall grant unto yow, profes, instructe, and mantene the purity of the doctrine, conteined in the sacred Word of God? And, to the uttermost of your power, will ye not ganestand and convince the gaynsayers and teichers of mennis inventiouns?

Answer.—That I do promeis in the presence of God, and of his congregatioun heir assembled.

Questioun.—Knaw ye not, that the excellency of this office, to the quhilk God hes called yow, requires that your conversatioun and behaviour be sick, as that ye may be irreprehensible; yea, even in the eyis of the ungodly?

Answer.—I unfaynedly acknawlege, and humilly desyre the Kirk of God to pray with me, that my lyfe be not scandalous to the glorious Evangell of Jesus Christ.

Questioun.—Becaus ye are a man compassed with infirmities, will ye not charitably, and with lawlines of spirit, receave admonitioun of your Brethrein? And if ye sall happin to slyde, or offend in ony point, will ye not be subject to the Discipline of the Kirk, as the rest of your Brethrein?

The Answer of the Superintendent, or Minister to be elected.

I acknawlege myself to be a man subject to infirmity, and ane that hes neid of correctioun and admonitioun; and tharefoir I maist willingly submit and subject my self to the hailsume disciplin of the Kirk; yea, to the discipline of the same Kirk by the quhilk I ame now called to this office and chairge; and heir in God's presens and youris do promeis obedience to all admonitiones, secretly or publickly gevin; unto the quhilk, if I be found inobedient, I confes myself most worthie to be ejected not onely from this honour, bot also frome the society of the Faythfull, in cais of my stubburnness: For the vocatioun of God to bear charge within his Kirk, makethe not men tyrantes, nor lordis, but appoynteth thame Servandis, Watchemen, and Pastoris of the Flock.

THE SUPERINTENDENT. 29

This ended, Questioun man be asked agane of the Multitude.

Question.—Require ye ony farther of this your Superintendent?

If no man answer, let the Minister proceid.

Will ye not acknawlege this your Brother, for the Minister of Christ Jesus? Will ye not reverence the word of God that proceids fra his mouthe? Will ye not receave of him the sermone of exhortatioun with patience, not refuising the hailsome medicine of your saules, althocht it be bitter and unpleising to the flesche? Will ye not finally, mantene and comforte him in his ministry, against all sick as wickedly wald rebell against God and his holy ordinance?

The Peple answereth.

We will, as we will answer to the Lord Jesus, quho hes commandit his Ministeris to be had in reverence, as his ambassadours, and as men that cairfully watche for the salvatioun of our saullis.

Let the Nobility also be urged with this.

Ye have heard the dewty and professioun of this your Brother, by your consentis appointit to this charge; as also the dewty and obedience, quhilk God requireth of us towards him heir in his ministry: Bot becaus that neyther of bothe are abill to performe ony thing without the especiall grace of our God in Christ Jesus, quho hes promeised to be with us present, even to the consummatioun of the world; with unfayned hairtis, let us crave of him his benedictioun and assistance in this work begun to his glory, and for the comfort of his Kirk.

The Prayer.

O LORD, to quhome all power is gevin in heavin and in eirthe, thow that art the Eternall Sone of the Eternall Father, quho hes not onely so luifit thy Kirk, that for the redemptioun and purgatioun of the same, thow hes humilled thyself to the deyth of the Croce; and thareupoun hes sched thy most innocent bluid, to prepair to thyself a Spous without spott; bot also, to retein this thy most excellent benefite in memory, hes appointed in thy Kirk, Teichears, Pastores, and Apostles, to instruct, comfort, and admonische the same: Luk upoun us mercifully, O Lord, thow that onely art King, Teicher, and Hie Priest to thy awin flock; and send unto this our Brother, quhome in thy name we have chairged with the cheif cair of thy Kirk, within the boundis of Louthiane, sick portioun of thy Holy Spreit, as thareby he may rychtly devyde thy word to the instructioun of thy flocke, and to the confutatioun of pernitious erroures, and damnable superstitiones. Give unto him, gude Lord, a mouthe and wisdome, quhareby the enemies of thy truthe may be confounded, the wolfis expellit, and driven from thy fauld, thy scheip may be fed in the wholsum pastures of thy most holy word, the blind and ignorant may be illuminated with thy trew knawlege: Finally, That the dregis of superstitioun and idolatry quhilk yit restis within this Realme, being purged and removed, we may all not only have occasioun to glorifie thee our onely Lord and Saviour, but also dayly to grow in godlines and obedience of thy most holy will, to the destructioun of the body of synne, and to the restitutioun of that image to the quhilk we wer anes created, and to the quhilk, efter our fall and defectioun, we ar renewed by participatioun of thy Holy Spirit, quhilk by trew fayth in thee, we do profes as the blessit of thy Father, of quhome the perpetuall incres of thy graces we crave, as by thee our Lord and King, and onely Bischope, we are taucht to pray, saying, " Our Father that art in hevin, &c."

The prayer ended, the rest of the Ministers, if ony be, and Elders of that Kirk present, in signe of thair consents, sall tak the elected by the hand, and then the cheif Minister sall gif the benedictioun as follows :—

GOD, the Father of our Lord Jesus Christ, quho hes commanded his Evangell to be preiched, to the comfort of his Elect, and hes called thee to the office of a Watchman over his

peple, multiply his graces with thee, illuminat
thee with his Holy Spirit, comfort and strenthen
thee in all vertewe, governe and guyde thy
ministry, to the prayse of his holy Name, to the
propagatioun of Christis kingdome, to the comforte of his Kirk, and finally, to the plain dischairge and assurance of thy awin conscience in
the day of the Lord Jesus; to quhome, with the
Father, and the Holy Ghost, be all honour,
prayse, and glory, now and ever. So be it.

The Last Exhortatioun to the Elected.

Take heid to thy self, and unto the Flock comitted to thy chairge; feid the same cairfully,
not as it wer of compulsioun, bot of very love,
quhilk thow bearest to the Lord Jesus. Walk
in simplicity and purenes of lyfe, as it becumethe
the trew servand and ambassadour of the Lord
Jesus. Usurpe not dominioun nor tyrranicall
impyre over thy brethrein. Be not discouraged
in adversity, bot lay befoir thyself the example
of Propheits, Apostles, and of the Lord Jesus,
quho in thair ministry susteaned contradictioun,
contempt, persecutioun and deyth. Feir not
to rebuik the warld of sinne, justice, and jugement. If ony thing succeid prosperously in thy
vocatioun, be not puft upe with pryde; nether yit
flatter thy self as that the gude succes proceided
from thy vertew, industry, or cair: Bot let ever
that sentence of the Apostle remaine in thy hairt;
" Quhat hes thou, quhilk thou hes not receavit ?

If thou hes receivit, quhy gloriest thou?" Comfort the afflicted, support the puir, and exhort utheris to support thame. Be not solist for things of this lyfe, bot be fervent in prayer to God for incress of his Holy Spirit. And finally, behave thyself in this holy vocatioun, with sick sobriety, as God may be glorified in thy ministry: And so sall thow schortly obtein the victory, and shall receave the crown promeised, quhen the Lord Jesus sall appeir in his glory, quhois Omnipotent Spirit assist thee and us unto the end. AMEN.

Then sing the 23d Psalme.

The Order

OF

The Ecclesiasticall Discipline.

As no Citie, Towne, howse, or familie can maynteine their estate and prospere without policie and governaunce, so the Churche of God, which requireth more purely to be governed then any citie or familie, can not without spirituall Policie and ecclesiasticall Discipline continewe, encrease, and florishe.

And as the Word of God is the life and soule of this Churche, so this godlie ordre and discipline is as it were synewes in the bodie, which knit and joyne the membres together with decent order and comelynes. It is a brydle to staye the wicked frome their myschiefes. It is a spurre to pricke forward suche as be slowe and necligent; yea, and for all men it is the Father's rodde ever in a readines to chastice gentelye the fautes committed, and to cawse theym afterward to lyve in more godlie feare and reverence. Finallye, it is an ordre left by God unto his Churche, wherby men learne to frame their wills, and doinges, accordinge to the lawe of God, by instructing and admonishinge one an other, yea, and by correctinge and ponishinge all obstinate rebells, and contemners of the same.

There are three cawses chiefly which move the Churche of God to the executinge of Discipline. First, that men of evell conversation be not nombred amongest God's childrene to their Father's reproche, as if the Churche of God were a sanctuary for naughtie and vile persons. The second respect is, that the good be not infected with compagnyinge the evell; which thinge S. Paule forsawe when he commaunded the Corinthians to banishe frome amongst theym the incestuous adulterer, sainge, "A litle leavyn maketh sowre the whole lump of dowe." The third cawse is, that a man thus corrected or excommunicated, might be ashamed of his faut, and so through repentance come to amendement; the which thinge the Apostole calleth, "deliveringe to Satan, that his soule may be saved in the day of the Lord;" meaning that he might be ponished with excommunication, to the intent his soule shuld not perishe for ever.

First, therfore, it is to be noted, that this censure, correction, or Discipline, is either private or publike; private, as if a man committ either in maners or doctrine against thee, to admonishe hym brotherly betwixt him and thee. If perchaunce he stubburnely resist thy charitable advertisementes, or els by contynuance in his faut declare that he amendeth not; then, after he hath bene the second tyme warned in presence of two or three witnesses, and continueth obstinately in his error, he oght, as our Savior Christ commaundeth, to be disclosed and uttered to the Church, so that accordinge to publike Discipline, he either may be receyved through repentance, or els be ponished as his faut requireth.

And here, as towchinge private Discipline, thre thinges are to be noted. First, that our admonitions procede of a godly zeale and conscience, rather sekinge to wynne our brother then to slaunder him. Next, that we be assured that his faut be reprouvable by God's Woord. And finally, that we use suche modestie and wisdome, that if we somewhat dout of the matter wherof we admonishe hym, yet with godly exhortations he may be broght to the knowlage of his faut. Or if the faut apperteyne to many, or be knowen of divers, that our admonition be done in presence of theym.

Briefly, if it concerne the whole Churche, in such sorte that the concelinge therof might procure some daunger to the same, that then it be uttered to the ministers and seniors, to whome the policie of the church doth apperteine.

Also in publike Disciplinè, it is to be observed that the Ministerie pretermit nothinge at any tyme unchastised with one kind of ponishement or other. If they perceyve any thinge in the Congregation, either evyll in example, sclaunderous in maners, or not besemynge their profession; as if there be any covetous personne, any adulterer, or fornicator, forsworne, thief, briber, false witnes-bearer, blasphemer, dronkarde, slaunderer, usurer; any person disobedient, seditious, or dissolute; any heresie or sect, as Papisticall, Anabaptisticall, and such like: briefly, whatsoever it be that might spott the Christian congregation, yea, rather whatsoever is not to edification, oght not to escape either admonition or ponishement.

And becawse it happeneth sometyme in the Churche of Christ, that when other remedies assayed proffitt nothinge, they must procede to the Apostolicall rodd and correction as unto Excommunication (which is the greatest and last ponishement belonginge to the spirituall Ministerie); it is ordeyned, that nothinge be attempted in that behalf with out the determination of the whole Churche: wherein also they must be ware and take good heede, that they seme not more readie to expell frome the Congregation then to receyve againe those in whome they perceyve worthie frutes of repentance to appeare. Neither yet to forbyd hym the hearinge of sermons, which is excluded frome the sacraments, and other duties of the Churche, that he may have libertie and occasion to repent. Finally, that all ponishementes, corrections, censures, and admonitions, stretche no farther then God's Woorde, with mercie, may lawfully beare.

MATTH. XVIII.

If any refuse to heare the Congregation, let him be as a heathen, and as a publicane.

The Order of Excommunication,
and of
Public Repentance.

To the Reader.

Albeit that in the Booke of Discipline the causes als weill of publict Repentance as of Excommunitioun, ar sufficientlie expressed : Yit because the Forme and Ordour ar not so set furth, that everic Church and Minister may have assurance that they agree with utheris in proceiding, it is thoght expedient to drawe that Ordour which universallie within this Realme shal be observed.

And First, we man understand what Crymes be worthie of Excommunicatioun, and what of publict Repentance.

In the First, it is to be noted, that all crymes that be the law of God deserve death, deserve also Excommunicatioun from the societie of Christis Church, whither the offendar be Papist or Protestant : For it is no reason that, under pretence of diversitie of religioun, open impiety shuld be suffered in the visible body of Christ Jesus; and thairfor wilfull murtherars, adulteraris (lauchfullie convict), sorcerars, witches, conjurars, charmars, and gevars of drinks to destroy children, and opin blasphemars (as if ony renunce God, deny the trueth and the authority of his Holie Word,

EXCOMMUNICATION.

rayll aganis his blessed Sacramentis), such, we say, aucht to be Excommunicat from the society of Christis Church, that their impiety may be haldin in greater horror, and that they may be the moir deiply wounded, perceaving themselfes abhorred of the godly. Aganis such opin malefactoris, the processe may be summar: For the cryme being knawin, advertisement aucht to be gevin to the Superintendent of the diocey, either be the Minister, or be such as can best geve informatioun of that fact; except in reformed townis and uther places where the Ministerie is planted with Minister and Eldaris, according to the Act of the General Assembly made the 26 of December 1568. And if there be no Superintendent where the cryme is committed, then aucht the informatioun to pas from such as ar offended to the nixt Superintendent, who with expeditioun aucht to direct his letters of summonds to the parish church where the offendar hath his residence, if the Ministerie be there planted : and if it be not, or if the offendar have no certane dwelling-place, then aucht the summonds to be direct to the cheife town, and best Reformed Church in that diocy, where the cryme was committed, appointing to the offendar a certain day, time, and place, where and when he shall compeire befoir the Superintendent and his assessors, to heare that cryme tried, as tuiching the trueth of it, and to answer for himself, why the sentence of Excommunicatioun should not be pronunced publiklie againis him. If the offendar,

lauchfullie warned, compeire not, inquisitioun
being takin of the cryme, charge may be gevin be
the Superintendent to the Ministers, so many as
shall be thoucht necessar for publicatioun of that
sentence, to pronunce the same the nixt Sunday,
the forme whereof shall after be declared : Bot
and if the offendar compeire and alledge for himselfe ony reasonable defence, to wit, that he will
not be fugitive from the law, but will abyde the
censure thereof for that offence, then may the
sentence of Excommunicatioun be suspendit till
that the magistrat be required to try that cause ;
wherein if the magistrats be negligent, then aucht
the Church from secret inquisition to proceid till
publique admonitioun, that the magistratis may
be vigilant in that cause of blood, which cryith
vengeance upon the hole land where it is sched
without punishment. If no remedie be them can
be found, then justly may the Church pronunce
the offendar excommunicat, as one suspect, besidis
his cryme, to have corrupted the judges, revengeris
of the blood : And so aught the Church to
proceid to Excommunication, whither the
offendar be fugitive from the law, or if he
procure pardoun, or elude the severity of justice
by means whatsoever besydis the tryal of his
innocencie.

If the offender abyde an assise, and by the
same be absolved, then may not the Church pronunce excommunicatioun, bot justlie may exhort
the man be whose hand the blood was sched, to
enter into consideration with himself, how pre-

EXCOMMUNICATION. 41

tious is the lyfe of man before God, and how severely God commandeth blood, (howsoever it be sched, except it be by the sword of the Magistrate) to be punished; and so may injoine unto him such satisfactionis to be made publikly to the Church, as may bear testificatioun of his obedience and unfained repentance. If the offendar be convict, and execution follow according to the cryme, then, upon the humble sute of him that is to suffer, may the Eldars and Ministers of the Church not only geve unto him consolatioun, bot also pronunce the sentence of absolutioun, and his sin to be remitted according to his repentance and faith. And thus much for Excommunication of publike Offendars.

And yit farther, we must considdir, that if the offendar be fugitive from the Law, so that punishment cannot be executed againis him, in that caise the Church aucht to delay no time, bot upon the notorietie of his cryme, and that he is fled from the presence of the judge, it aucht to pronunce him excommunicated publikly, and so continually to repute him, untill such tyme that the magistrat be satisfied: And so whither the offendar be convict in judgment, or be fugitive from the Law, the Church aucht to proceid to the sentence of Excommunicatioun; the Forme whereof followeth:—

The Minister, in publike audience of the Pepill sall say,—

It is cleirlie knawin unto us that N., sometymes baptized in the Name of the Father, and of the Sone, and of the Holy Ghost, and so reputed and compted for a Christian, hath fearfullie fallin from the society of Christ's body, by committing of cruell and wilful murther (or by committing filthy adultery, &c.), which cryme be the law of God deserveth death: And because the civil sword is in the hand of God's Magistrat, who notwithstanding oft winkis at such crymes, we having place in the Ministery, with grief and dolour of our harts, ar compelled to draw the sword granted be God to his Church; that is, to Excommunicat from the society of Christ Jesus, from his body the Church, from participatioun of sacraments, and prayers with the same, the said N. AND THEREFORE, IN THE NAME AND AUTHORITIE OF THE ETERNAL GOD, AND OF HIS SON JESUS CHRIST, We pronunce the said N. excommunicate and accursed in this his wicked fact; and charge all that favor the Lord Jesus so to repute and hold him (or hir) untill such time as that either the Magistrat have punished the offendar as Goddis law commandis, or that the same offendar be reconciled to the Church again be publique repentance: And in the mean tyme we earnestlie desire all the faithful to call upon God to move the harts of the upper powers so to punish such horrible crymes, that malefactors may fear to offend, evin for feare of punishment; and also so to tuich the hart of the offendar, that he may deipelie consider how fearefull it is to fall in the hands of the eternal God, that by unfained repentance he may apprehend mercie in

EXCOMMUNICATION.

Jesus Christ, and so avoid eternal condemnatioun.

The sentence of Excommunicatioun ones pronunced, the Church may not suddanly admit the murtherar, or convict adulterar, to repentance and society of the faithfull, albeit that pardon be purchased of the Magistrat; bot first aucht inquisition to be taken if the murtherar have satisfied the party offended, that is, the kin and friendis of the man slain; which if he hath not done, neither is understood willing so to do, the Church in no wayis may heare him. Bot if he be willing to satisfie, and the freinds exceid measure and the possibilitie of him that hath committed the cryme, then aucht the Church to put moderatioun to the unreasonable, incaise the Civil magistrat hath not so done befoir, and so proceid with him that offereth repentance, that the wilfulnes of the indiscreit be not hinderance to the reconciliatioun of him that earnestlie craveth the benefit and society of the Church.

And yit may not the Church receave ony Excommunicat at his first requeist; bot in such grevous crymes as befoir ar expressed (of utheris shall be efter spokin), fourty dayis at the least after his first offer may be appointed, to try whither the signes of repentance appeir in the offendar or not. And yit in the mean tyme the Church may confort him be holsome admonitiouns, assuring him of God's mercy, if he be verily penitent; he may also be admitted to the hearing of the Word; bot in no wyse to participatioun of prayeris, nether befoir nor efter the sermon. The first fourty dayis expyred, upon his new suit, the Superintendent or Sessioun may injoyne such paines as may try whether he be penitent or not: The least ar, the murtherar man stand three several Sundayis in a publike place before the church dore bare-futed and bare-headed, cled in a base and abject apparrell, having the same weapen which he used in the murther, or the lyke, bloody in his hand, and in conceaved words shall say to such as shall enter into the church :—

The Confessioun of the Penitent.

So farre hath Sathan gottin victorie ovir me, that cruelly I have sched innocent blood, for the which I have deserved death corporall and eternall ; and so I grant my selfe unworthy of the common light, or yit of the companie of men : And yit because in God there is mercy that passeth all measure, and because the Magistrat hath not takin from me this wretchit lyfe, I most earnestlie desyre to be reconciled again with the Church of Christ Jesus, from the societie whereof mine iniquitie hath caused me to be excommunicated ; and therefore, in the bowelis of Christ Jesus, I crave of you to pray with me unto God, that my grevous cryme may be of him remitted, and also that ye will be suppliants with me to the Church, that I abyd not thus Excommunicat unto the end.

At the last of the three Sundayis certain of the Eldaris shall receive him into the Church, and present him before the preaching place, and shall declair unto the Minister, that all that was injoyned to that offendar was obedientlie fulfilled by him. Then shall the Minister recite unto him als well the grevousnes of his sin, as the mercies of God, if he be penitent. And therefter shall require of the Church, If that they desire any farther satisfactioun ? And if no answer be gevin, then shall the Minister pronunce his sin to be remitted according to his repentance, and shall exhort the Church to embrace him as a brother, efter that prayer and thankisgeving be gevin unto God, as efter shall be descryved.

And thus far to be observed for the Ordour in receaving of thame that have committed capital crymes, be it murther, adulterie, incest, witchcraft, or utheris befoir expressed.

Apostates to Papistrie.

Resteth yit one uther kynd of offendaris that deserve Excommunicatioun, albeit not so summarlie, to wit, such as have bene partakers with us in doctrine and sacraments, and have returned back agane to the Papistrie, or have gevin their presence to onie part of their abhominatioun, or yit that of onie long continuance, withdrawe themselfis from the societie of Christis bodie, and from the participatioun of the sacramentis, when they ar publiklie ministred. Such, no doubt, declair themselfis worthie of excommunicatioun; bot first they man be called either befoir the Superintendent, with sum joyned with him, or elis befoir the Eldaris and Sessioun of the best and nixt Reformed Church where the offendaris have their residence, who man accuse their defectioun, exhort them to repentance, and declair to them the danger wherein they stand.

Whom if the offendar hearith, the Sessioun or Superintendent may appoynt him ane day to satisfie the Church publikelie, whom by his defectioun he had offended. Bot if he continue stubburne, then may the Sessioun or Superintendent command the Minister or Ministers to declair the next Sunday the defectioun of such ane person, and his obstinate contempt; and this advertisement being gevin two Sundayis, the third may the sentence of Excommunication be pronunced.

Offences that deserve publike Repentance, and Order to proceide thereintill.

Such offences as fall not under the Civile sword, and yit ar sclanderous and offensive in the Church, deserve publike Repentance: and of these sum ar more haynous than utheris,— fornication, drunkennes used, swearing, cursed speaking, chyding, feghting, brawling, and commoun contempt of the ordor of the Church, breaking of the Sabbath, and such like, aucht to

PUBLIC REPENTANCE. 47

be in no person suffered : Bot the sclander being knawin, the offendar should be called befoir the Ministery, his cryme provin, accused, rebuked, and he commanded publiklie to satisfie the Church; which if the offendar refuis, they may proceid to Excommunicatioun, as efter shall be declaired. If the offendar compeir not, summonds aucht to pass to the third time ; and then incase he compeir not, the Church may decerne the sentence to be pronunced.

Utheris be less haynous, and yit deserve admonition, as wanton and vain words, uncomelie gestures, negligence in hearing the preachingis, or abstening from the Lordis Table, when it is publiklie ministrat, suspicioun of avarice or of pryde, superfluitie or ryotousnes in cheir or rayment ; these, we say, and such utheris, that of the world are not regarded, deserve admonitioun amongis the membres of Christis body : First, secretly, by one or two of those that first espy the offence, which if the person suspected hear, and geve declaratioun of amendment, then there nedeth no farther proces.

Bot if he contempne and despiseth admonitioun, then shuld the former admonisaris tak to themselfis two or three faithful and honest witnesses, in whose presence the suspected offendar shuld be admonished, and the causes of their suspitioun declaired ; to whom if then he geve significatioun of repentance, and promise of amendment, they may cut off all farther accusatioun : Bot and if he obstinately contempne both the said admonitiouns, then aucht the first and second brethren to signifie the matter to the Ministers and Eldaris in their Sessioun, who aucht to call the offendar, and, before the complainars, accuse him als weill of the cryme, as of the contempt of the admonitioun. If then he acknawledge his offence, and be willing to satisfie the brethren befoir offended, and the Sessioun then present, there nedeth no farther publication of the offence.

Bot if he declair himself inobedient to the Session, then without delay the nixt Sunday aucht the cryme, and the ordor of admonitionis passed befoir, be publiklie declaired to the Church, and the person (without specificatioun of his name) be admonished to satisfie in publique that which he refused to do in secret: And that for the first. If he offerris himself to the Church, befoir the nixt Sunday, the discretioun of the Ministerie may tak such ordor, as may satisfie als weill the private personis that first war offended, as the Church, declairing the repentance and submissioun of that brother, that befoir appeared stubburne and incorrigible.

Bot and if he abyde the second publict admonitioun, when that his name shall be expressed, and his offences and stubburnnes declared, then can no satisfactioun be receaved bot in publict; yea, it may not be receaved befoir that he have humblie required the same of the Ministerie and Sessioun of the Church in their appointed Assemblie.

PUBLIC REPENTANCE.

If he continue stubburne, then the third Sunday aucht he to be charged publiklie to satisfie the Church for his offence and contempt, under the pain of Excommunication; the Order whereof shall efter be declaired. And thus a small offence or sclander may justly deserve Excommunication, by reason of the contempt and disobedience of the offendar. If the offendar schaw himself penitent betwene the first admonitioun and the second, and satisfie the Ministerie of the Church, and the brethren that were befoir offended in their Assemblie, then it may suffice that the Minister, at commandement of the Sessioun, declair the nixt Sunday (without compeiring or expressing of the person) his repentance and submission in these or uther wordis:—

It was signified unto you befoir, deirlie belovit, that one certan brother (or brethren) was noted, or at least suspected of some offence wherof he being admonished by one or two, appeared lightlie to regard the same; and therefoir was he and his offence notified unto the Ministerie in their Assembly, who, according to their deuty and charge, accused him of the same; and not finding in him such obedience as the professioun of ane Christian requireth, fearing that such offences and stubburnnes shuld engender contempt, and infect utheris, they war compelled to notifie unto you the cryme and the proceidingis of the Sessioun, mynding to have soucht the uttermost remedie incase the offendar had continued obstinate. Bot seeing that it hath pleased God to mollifie the hart of our brother, whose name we neid not to expresse, so that he hath not onlie acknowledged his offence, bot also hath fullie satisfied the brethren that first war offended, and us the Ministerie, and hath promised to abstene from all appearance of such evill, as whereof he was suspected and admonished, we have no just cause to proceid to ony farther extremitie, but rather to glorifie God for the submissioun of our brother, and unfainedlie pray unto him, that in the lyke caise we and everie one of us may geve the lyke obedience.

The Forme of Publique Repentance.

It is first to be observed, that none may be admitted to publique repentance except that first they be admitted thereto be the Sessioun and Assemblie of the Ministeris and Eldaris; in the which they aucht sharplie to be examinat, what feire and terrour they have of God's judgmentis, what hatred of sin, and dolour for the same, and what sense and feiling they have of God's mercies: In the which if they be ignorant, they aucht diligently to be instructed; for it is but ane mocking to present such to publik repentance, as neither understand what sin is, what repentance is, what grace is, nor be whom God's favour and mercie is purchased. After then that the offendar shall be instructed in the Assemblie, so that to have sum taist of God's judgements, bot

PUBLIC REPENTANCE.

chiefly of God's mercies in Christ Jesus, he may be presented before the publik Church upon a Sunday after the sermon, and before the Prayeris and Psalme, and then the Minister shall say,—

Beloved and dearest Brethren, we, be reason of our charge and Ministery, present befoir you this brother, that by the infirmitie of the flesh and craft of Sathan, hes feirfullie fallen from the obedience of his God, by committing N. of a cryme, &c. (let the sin be expressed); by the which he hes not only offended against the Majestie of God, bot also by the same hes gevin great sclander and offence till his holy congregatioun; and therefore doeth till his owin confusion (bot to the glorie of God and our great confort) present himself here before you, to witnes and declair his unfained repentance, the thrist and the caire that he hes to be reconciled with God throw Jesus Christ, and with you his brethren, whom he hes offended : and therefore it is requisite that ye and he understand what assurance we have to requyre such publik satisfaction of him, what profit we aucht to learne in the same, and what profit and utilitie redoundes to both of this his humiliatioun.

That publik Repentance is the institutioun of God, and not man's invention, may be plainly gaddered of the words of our Maister, commanding, "that if ony have offended his brother, in what sort so ever it be, that he shall go to him and be reconciled unto his brother." If the offence committed against one brother requyres reconciliatioun, the offence committed against many brethren requires the same. And if a man be charged be Christ Jesus to go to a man whom he has offended, and thair be confessioun of his offence requyre reconciliatioun, much moir is he bound to seik a whole multitude whom he hes offended, and befoir them with all humility requyre the same ; for that wo which our Maister Christ Jesus pronunceth against every man that hes offended the least one within his Church, remaneth upon every publik offendar untill such tyme as he declair himself willing to remove the same, which he can never do untill such tyme as he let the multitude whom he hes offended understand his unfained repentance.

But because that all men of upricht judgment agree in this, that publik offences requyre publik repentance, we pass to the second head, which is, What it is that we have to consider in the fall and sin of this our brother. If we consider his fall and sin in him only, without having consideration of our selfis, and of our owin corruption, we shall profit nothing, for so shall we bot despyse our brother and flatter our selfis. But if we shall earnestlie consider what nature we bear, what corruption lurketh in it, how prone and readie everie one of us is to such and greater impietie, then shall we in the sinne of this our brother accuse and damne our owin sinnes, in his fall shall we consider and lament our sinful nature; also shall we joyne our repentance, teares, and prayeris with him and his, knowing that no flesh can be justified before God's presence, if judgement proceid without mercie. The profit which this our brother and we have of this his humiliation, is, that we and he may be assured that our God is moir reddie to receave us to mercie, through Jesus Christ his only Sone, then we ar to crave it. It is not sinne, be it never so grevous, that shall debar us from his favour, if we seik to his mercie ; for as all have sinned, and ar by themselfis destitute of God's grace, so is he reddie to shaw mercie unto all that unfainedlie call for the same ; yea, he doth not onlie receave such as come, but he, by the mouth of his deir Sone, calleth upon such as be burdened and laidened with sinne, and solemnedlie promiseth that he will refresh them.

We have besides ane uther commoditie, to wit, that if we shall heirefter fall into the lyke or greater (for we stand not by our owin power, but by grace only), that we be not eschamed in this same sort to humble our selfis and confesse our offence. Now, therefore, brother, as we all praise God in this your humiliatioun, beseiking him that it be without hypocrisie, so it becummeth ye earnestly to considder of what mind and with what hart ye present your self heir before this Assemblie. It is not your sine that shall separate you from your God, nor from his mercy in Jesus Christ, if ye repent the same ; bot hypocrisie and impenitencie, which God remove from you and us, is nowise tolerable before his presence.

The Offendar aucht to protest before God, that he is sory for his sinne, and unfainedly desyreth God to be mercifull unto him, and that for the obedience of his deir Sone our Lord Jesus Christ.

The Minister.

We can only see that which is without, and according to your confessioun judge, leaving the secretis of the hart to God, who only can try and search the same. Bot because unfeaned repentance for sinne, and simple confessioun of the same, ar the mere giftis of God, we will joyne our prayeris with youris, that the one and the uther may be granted to you and us.

The Prayer.

Eternal and everliving God, Father of our Lord Jesus Christ, thow that by the mouth of thy holy Propheites and Apostillis hes plainlie pronunced, that thow desyrest not the death of ane sinner, bot rather that he may convert and live; who also hes sent thy only Sone to suffer the cruell death of the croce, not for the just, but for such as find themselfis oppressed with the burden of sinne, that by him and his advocation they may have acces to the throne of thy grace, being assured, that before thee they shall find favour and mercy: We are convened, O Lord, in thy presence, and that in the Name of this same our Lord Jesus thy deir Sone, to accuse before thee our sinnes, and before the feit of thy

PUBLIC REPENTANCE. 55

Majesty, to crave mercy for the same. We most humbly beseche thee, O Father of Mercies, first, that thou wilt tuich and move our harts by the power of thy Holy Spirit, in such sort, that we may come to ane trew knawledge of our sinnes; bot chiefly, O Lord, it will please thee to move the hart of this our brother N., &c., who, as he hes offended thy Majesty, and ane great number of this thy holy congregation, by his grevous and publik sine, so doeth he not refuse publikly to acknawledge and confesse the same, as that this his humiliatioun gevin to the glory of thy Name presently doeth witnes. Bot because, O Lord, the external confessioun, without the dolour of the hart, availeth nothing in thy presence, we most humblie beseche thee, that thou wilt so effectually move his hart, and ouris also, that he and we without hypocrisie, damning that which thy law pronunceth injust, may atteine to some sense and feiling of thy mercy, which thou hast abundantly shawen unto mankynd in Jesus Christ our Lord.

Grant, O Lord, unto this our brother, the repentance of the hart, and sincere confession of the mouth, to the praise of thy Name, to the confort of thy Church, and to the confusion of Sathan. And unto us grant, O Lord, that albeit we cannot live altogether cleine of sinne, yit that we fall not in horrible crymes to the dishonor of thy holy Name, to the sclander of our brethren, and infamy of thy holy Evangel, which we professe. Let thy godly power, O Lord, so strengthen our weaknes, that nether the craft of Sathan, nor the tyranny of sinne, draw us utterly from thy obedience. Give us grace, O Lord, that by holines and innocencie of lyfe, we may declaire to this wicked generatioun what difference there is betwixt the sones of light and the sones of darknes; that men seeing our gud workis, may glorify thee, and thy Sone Jesus Christ, our only Saviour and Redemer; to whom with Thee, and the Holy Spirit, be all honor praise, and glory, now and ever. Amen.

The Prayer finished, the Minister shall turne him to the Penitent brother, and in full audience shall say:—

You have heard, brother, what is your dewtie towardes the Church, which ye have offended, to wit, that willingly ye confesse that cryme that you have committed, asking God mercie for the same, and so that ye may reconcile your self to the Church which ye have offended. You have hard also the affection and care of the Church towardes you their penitent brother, notwithstanding your grevous fall, to wit, that we all heir present joyne our sinnes with your sinne; we all repute and esteime your fall to be our owen; we accuse our selfis no less then we accuse you. Now, finally, we joyne our prayeris with youris, that we and ye may obtene mercy, and that by the means of our Lord Jesus Christ. Let us, therefore, brother, have this confort of you, that

PUBLIC REPENTANCE.

ye wil openlie and simplie confesse your cryme, and give to us attestation of your unfained repentance.

The Penitent shall then openlie confesse the cryme, whatsoever it be, and shall desyre God's mercie, and pray the Church to call to God for mercie with him, and unfainedly desyre that he may be joyned againe to their society and number.

If the Penitent be confounded with shame, or such ane one as cannot distinctlie speik to the confort and instruction of the Church, the Minister shall mak repetition, that every head may be understood by it self, and thereafter shall ask the penitent if that be his confession, and if so he beleveth. His answer affirmative being receaved, the Minister shall ask the congregation if they judge any farther to be requyred for their satisfactioun and reconciliation of that brother. No contradictioun being made, the Minister shall say to the Penitent :—

We have heard, deir brother, your confession, for the which we from our hartis praise God ; for in it the Spirit of Jesus Christ hath confounded the Devill, and broken down his head and power, in that, that you, to the glorie of God, have openly damned your self and your impiety, imploring grace and mercie for Christ Jesus his Sones sake. This strenth, submission and obedience, cannot proceid from flesh and blude, but is the singular gift of the Holy Ghost: acknowledge, therefore, it to be gevin unto you by Jesus Christ our Lord; and now tak heed, lest at any tyme ye be unmyndfull of this great benefit, which no doubt Sathan doth invy, and will assaile by all means possible, that you may abuse it. He will not cease to tempt you to fall againe in such, or crymes more horrible; bot resist the devill, and he shall flee from you. Live in sobrietie; be instant in prayer, commend your self unfainedly to God, who as he is faithfull, so shall he give to us victorie over sinne, death, and Sathan, and that by means of our Head and soveraigne champion Jesus Christ; to whom be all praise, glory, and honour, now and ever. Amen.

Ane Admonition to the Church.

It is your dewtie, Brethren, to tak example of this our penitent brother: First, That ye be unfainedly displeased in your own harts for your sinnes: Secondarly, That with this our brother ye accuse them in the sight of God, imploring grace and mercie for your offences committed: And last, if any of you shall after this publikly offend, that ye refuse not with the like reverence to satisfie the Church of God, offended in you. Now only resteth, that ye remit and foryet all offences which ye have conceaved heretofore by the sinne and fall of this our brother; accept and embrace him as ane member of Christ's body; let none tak upon him to reproche or accuse him for any offences, that before this hour he hath committed. And that he may have the better assurance of your good will and reconciliation, prostrate your selfis before God, and render him thanks for the conversion and repentance of this our brother.

The Thanksgeving.

Heavenly Father, Fountaine of all mercy and consolation, we confesse our selves unworthy to be counted amongis thy children, if thou have respect to the corruption of our nature; but seeing it hath pleased thy Fatherly goodnes, not only freely to chuse us in thy deir Sone our Lord Jesus Christ, by his death to redeme us, by his Evangel to call us, and by his Holy Spirit (which both are thine) to illuminate us ; but also that thou hast commanded thy Word and holie Evangel to be preached, to the end that the penitent shall have an assurance of the remission of their sinnes, not onlie for a tyme, bot even als oft as men from sorrowfull hartis shall call for thy grace and mercie. In consideration of this thy Fatherly adoption and ineffable clemencie shawen upon us, we cannot bot praise and magnifie thy Fatherlie mercie; an testimonie whereof we not onlie feile in our selfis, bot also see the same evidentlie in the conversion of this our brother, whom Sathan for an tyme held in bondage, bot now is set at freedome by the power of our Lord Jesus Christ, and is returned againe to the societie of his bodie. Grant unto us, heavenlie

Father, that he and we may more and more be displeased for our sinnes, and proceid in all manner of gud workis, to the praise of thy holy Name, and edification of thy Church, by Jesus Christ our Lord and only Saviour. So be it.

> *The Thankesgiving being finished, the Minister shall requyre of the Penitent, if that he will be subject to the Discipline of the Church, in caise that he after offend: Who answering that he will, the Minister shall say, in maner of Absolution:—*

If thou unfainedly repentis thy former iniquity, and beleves in the Lord Jesus, then I, in his Name, pronunce and affirme that thy sinnes ar forgevin, not only on earth, but also in heaven, according to the promises annexed with the preiching of his Word, and to the power put in the Ministerie of his Church.

> *Then shall the Eldaris and Deacons, with Ministers (if anie be), in the name of the hole Church, take the reconciled brother by the hand, and embrace him, in signe of full reconciliation.*
>
> *Then after shall the Church sing the CIII. Psalme, so much as they think expedient; and so shall the Assemblie, with the benediction, be dismissed.*

The Forme of Excommunication.

AFTER that all admonitions, both private and publict, be past, as before is said, then must the Church proceid to Excommunication, if the offender remain obstinate. The Sunday, therefore, after the thrid publik admonition, the Minister being before charged by the Session or Elders, shall thus signify unto the Church after the sermon:

It is not unknowen unto you, with what lenity and carefulnes the Ministerie and the whole Church, by private and publict admonitions, hath sought N., etc., to satisfie the Church, and to declare himself penitent for his grevous crymes and rebellion, by the which he hath offended God's Majestie, blasphemed his holie Name, and offended his Church; in whom to this day we finde nothing bot stubburnnes: We cannot, therefore, of conscience, wink anie longer at the disobedience of the saide N., lest that his example infect and hurt uthers: We are compelled, therefore, in the feare of God, to give the said N. into the hands and power of the devill, to the destruction of the flesh, if that by that meane he may be broght to the consideration of himself, and so repent and avoide that fearfull condemnation that shall fall on all inobedient in the day of the Lord Jesus. And lest that onie shuld think that we do this of manlie presumption, without the assurance of the Scriptures, ye shall shortlie hear what commandement and authoritie we have so to do.

First, We have the commandement of our Maister and Savionr Jesus Christ, to holde such for ethniks and publicanes as will not hear the voyce of the Church : but plaine it is, that this obstinate N. hath contemptuouslie refused all wholsome admonitions, and therefore we (not one or two, but the whole Church) must holde him as a publicane, that is, as one cut off from the bodie of Jesus Christ, and unworthie of anie societie with him, or with the benefites of his Church, till his new conversion and his receaving againe.

Secundarly, We have the command of the Apostle St. Paul, and that fearful sentence, which he, being absent, did notwithstanding pronunce against the incest, with his sharpe rebuke to the Corinthians, because that with greater zeale and expedition they expelled not from amonges them that wicked man. And if anie thinke that the offence of this foir-named obstinate is not so haynous as that of incest, let such understand, that mercie and favour may rather be graunted til anie uther sinne then to the contempt of holesome admonitions, and of the just and laughfull ordinances of the Church. For uther sinnes, how haynous so ever they be (so be it that they deserve not death), as by unfeaned repentance they ar remitted before God ; so upon the same humblie offered unto the Church, order may be

EXCOMMUNICATION. 63

taken, that the offendar may be conforted, and at lenth restored to the societie of the Church againe : but such as proudlie contempne the admonition of the Church, private or publike, declare themselfes stubburne, rebellious, and altogether impenitent, and therefore most justlie ought they to be Excommunicate.

The precept of God gevin under the law, to expell from the middes of God's people such as were leprous (without exception of persons), is to us an assurance that we ought to expell from the societie of Christ's body such as be striken with spiritual leprosie ; for the one is no lesse infective and dangerous then is the uther. Now, seeing that we know Excommunication is God's ordinance, let us in few words understand the utility and use of the same.

By it, first, the Church is purged of open wicked doers, which is no small commodity, considering that we feght in the middes and eyes of this wicked generation, which seiketh in us nothing more than occasion of sclander. Secondarly, By it is the Church and every member of the same reteaned in obedience and feare, whereof all have need, if the frailtie of our flesh shall be rightly considdered. Thirdly, By it we exercise ane singular worke of charity, while that we declare our selfes carefull to kepe the flock of Christ in purity of maners, and without danger to be infected : for, as it war a worke both uncharitable and cruell to joyne together in one bed persones infected with pestilent or uther contagious and infective sores, with tender children, or with such as war hole, so it is no lesse crueltie to suffer amonges the flock of Jesus Christ such uther obstinat rebelles : for trew is that sentence of the Apostle,—" A little leaven corrupteth the whole masse." But lest that we shuld seme to usurpe power owir the Church, or to doe any thing without the knowledge and consent of the whole body, for this present we delay the sentence, willing, such as have any thing to object in the contrair, to propone the same the nixt Session day, or eles to signify the same to some of the Ministeris or Eldaris, that answer may be gevin thereto ; and in the meane tyme we will call to God for the conversion of the impenitent.

A Prayer for the Obstinat.

Eternall and everliving God, Father of our Lord Jesus Christ, whose verie property is to shaw mercie, and to restore life, even when to man's judgement death hath gottin dominion over thy creatures: for thou first soght, called, accused, and convicted our father Adam after his transgression ; and being so dead in sinne, and thrall to Sathan, that he could nether confesse his offence, nor yit ask mercy for the same, thou by thy free promises of mercy and grace gave unto him a new lyfe and strenth to repent. The same ordor must thou kepe, O Lord, with all thy chosen children of his posteritie ; for in mannis

EXCOMMUNICATION. 65

corrupt nature there can be no obedience, whill that thou by operation of thy Holy Spirit worke the same. And therefore, we most humbly beseke thee, for Jesus Christ thy Sones sake, pitifullie to look upon this thy creature, who ones was baptized in thy Name, and hath professed himself subject to thy religioun and unto the discipline of thy Church, whome Sathan, alas, now so blyndeth, that obstinately he contemneth the one and the uther. We have followed, O Lord, the reule prescribed unto us by thy deir Sone our Lord Jesus Christ, in admonishing and threatning him; bot hidderto have profited nothing concerning him and his humiliation.

But, O Lord, as thou alone knowes, so may thou alone change and mollifie the harts of the proud and impenitent: thou, by the voce of thy Prophet Nathan, wakened David from his dedlie securitie: thou, without anie prophet, bet down the pryde of Manasses in the prison, after he had sched the blood of thy servandis, and had replenished Jerusalem with all kynd of impitie: thou turned the hart of Peter at the look of thy deir Sone our Lord Jesus Christ, efter that feirfullie, with horrible imprecationis, he had thrise openlie denied him.

O Lord, thy mercies without measure endure for evir, to the which we efter long travell do remit this obstinat and impenitent; earnestlie desiring thee, O Father of mercies, first so to peirse his hart with the feir of thy severe judgements, that he may begin to understand, that thus contemning all holesome admonitions, he provokis thy wraith and indignation againes himself. Open his eyis, that he may see how feirful and terrible a thing it is to fall into thy hands: and therefter mollifie and oynt his hart by the unction of thy Holy Spirit, that he may unfeanedly convert unto thee, and geve unto thee that honour and obedience that thou requirest in thy holy word; and so to our confort that now mourne for his rebellion, that he may subject himself to the just ordinance of thy Church, and avoide that feirfull vengeance that most assuredly shall fall upon all the inobedient. These thy graces, O heavenly Father, and farther, as thou knowest to be expedient for us, and for thy Church universall, we call for according as we are taught to pray be our soverane Maister, Christ Jesus, saying, OUR FATHER, &c.

The secund Sunday, efter the sermone and publict prayeris, the Minister shall, in audience of the hole Church, ask the Eldars and Deaconis,—who man sit in an eminent and proper place, that there answer may be heard—

The Minister.

Hath N., whom the last day we admonished, under the pain of Excommunication, to satisfie the Church for his publict sclander and contempt of the Ministerie, be himself, or be any uther, offered his obedience unto you?

EXCOMMUNICATION.

They shall answere as the Truth is, yea or nay.

If he hath soght the favoris of anie within the Ministerie, with promise of obedience, then shall farther process be delayed, and he commanded to appeir before the Sessioun in there nixt assemblie, where ordor may be takin for his publict repentance, as in the former head is expressed. If he have not labored to satisfie the Church, then shall the Minister proceid and say :

It can not but be dolorous to the bodie, that anie one membre thereof shuld be cut off and perish ; and yit it aucht to be more feirfull to the membre then to the bodie, for the membre cut off can doe nothing but putrifie and perish, and yit the bodie may reteine lyfe and strenth. Bot the rebellioun of this obstinat may proceid in one part from ignorance ; for it may be that he understandeth not what excommunication is, and what is the danger of the same; I shall therefoir in few wordes oppin the one and the uther.

Laughfull excommunication (for the thundringis of that Romane Antichrist ar bot vanity and wynd) is the cutting off from the body of Jesus Christ, from participatioun of his holy sacramentis, and from publict prayeris with his Church, be publike and solemned sentence, all obstinat and impenitent personis, efter dew admonitionis : which sentence, lawghfullie pronunced on earth, is ratified in heaven, by bynding of the same sinnes that they bynd on earth. The danger hereof is greater than man can suddanly espy; for seeing that without the body of Jesus Christ there abydeth nothing bot death and damnation to mankynd, in what estait shall we judge them to stand, that justly are cut off from the same?

Yea, what horrible vengeance hangeth upon them and their posteritie, notable and severe punishmentis may instruct us: Cain the murtherar was not accursed in his awin person only, bot that same malediction rang in his posteritie, and upon all that joyned therewith, till that all mankynd was destroyed by water (eight persons reserved). Cham lykewyse was accursed in his sone Canaan, the severity whereof proceded evin to the exterminion of that hole race and nation. The sempill word of our Maister Jesus Christ caused the figg-tree suddanly to wither. At the voyce of Peter, Ananias and Sapphira war striken to death. The same God and Lord Jesus, with the power of his Holie Spirit that then was potent and just, wirkis evin now in the Ministerie of his Church, the contempt whereof he will in no wyse suffer unpunished. And therefoir ye that have acquentance or familiarity with the foir-named obstinat, declair unto him these dangeris, and will him not to tempt the uttermoist. And thus yit again let us pray to God for his conversion.

Let the former Prayer be publictly said.

The thrid Sonday, let the first questioun be proponed by the Minister to the Eldaris and

EXCOMMUNICATION.

Deaconis, concerning the submission of the Obstinat, so oft admonished, as was proponed the second. If repentance be offered, let ordour be takin, as is befoir said, with a charge to the Church to prayse God for the conversion of that brother. If repentance be not offered, then shall the Minister expone wherein the persone that is to be Excommunicat hath offended, how oft and by whom he hath bene admonished, als weil privatelie as publictly ; and shall demand of the Eldaris and Deaconis if it be not so : Whose answer receaved, the Minister shall ask the hole Church if they think that such contempt shuld be suffered amonges them : and if then no man mak intercession for the obstinat, the Minister shall proceid, and say :—

Of very conscience we are compelled to do that which to our hartis is most dolorous, to wit, to geve over in the handis of the Devill, this foirnamed obstinat contemner N., whom ones we esteimed a membre of our body ; and that not onlie for the cryme that he hath committed, bot much rather for his proud contempt and intollerable rebellioun, lest that our sufferance of him in this his impietie shuld not only be imputed unto us, bot also that he shuld infect uthers with the same pestilence. And therefore we man use the last remedie, how grevous that ever it be unto us : and yit I desire you, for more ample declaratioun of your Christian charity towards him, ye pray with me unto God, now for the last, for his conversioun.

The last Prayer before the Excommunicatioun.

Omnipotent, Eternall, and Mercifull Father, who, for that good-will that thou bearest unto us in Jesus Christ thy deir Sone, wilt not the death and destruction of a sinner, but rather that he, by inspiration and moving of thy Holie Spirit, convert and live; who also doest witnes the vertew and strenth of thy word to be such, that it causeth the mountains to schaik, the rockes to tremble, and the floods to drie up; behald, we thy children and people here prostrat before thee, most humblie beseik thee, in the Name of thy deire Sone our Lord Jesus Christ, that thou wilt move and peirse the hart of our impenitent brother, whom Sathan so long hath indured and hardened; let it pleise thy Majestie, be the vertew of thy Holie Spirit, that thou wilt mollifie the same. Expell his darknes, and by the light of thy grace that thou wilt so illuminat him, that now at lenth he may feil, first, How grevously he hath offended againis thy Majestie: and, secondarly, againis thy holie Church and Assemblie. Give him thy grace to acknawledg, accuse, and damne als weil befoir us whom he hath offended, as befoir thy presence, this his proud contempt, lest that we, by the same provoked, be compelled, with all our griefis, to cut him off thy mysticall bodie, whom we, O Lord, unfeanedly desire to retene within thy Church, as a lyvely member of thy deir Sone our Lord Jesus. Heir us, merciful Father; call back again this

EXCOMMUNICATION.

our impenitent brother that now tendith to eternal destruction; that we al, who befoir thy presence evin for his rebellion do murne, may receave him again with gladnes and joy, and so render prayse and honour unto thee befoir this thy holie Congregatioun.

We grant our selfis, O Lord, unworthy whom thou should heir, because we cease not to offend thee by our continual transgression of thy holy precepts. Look not upon us, mercifull Father, in this our corrupt nature, bot look thou to thy deir Sone, whom thou of thy mere mercie hast appointed our Head, great Bishop, Advocat, Mediator, and only Propitiator. In him and in the merites of his death. We humblie beseche thee mercifullie to behald us, and suffer not the most innocent blude of thy deir Sone, sched for us, and for this our impenitent brother, to be prophaned by the tyranny and slight of Sathan. Bot, by the vertew of the same, let this our impenitent brother be broght to unfeaned repentance, that so he may escaip that feirfull condemnatioun, in the which he appeireth to fall. This we ask of thee, O heavenly Father, in the boldnes of our Head and Mediator Jesus Christ, praying as he hath taught us, OUR FATHER, &c.

If after this Prayer the Obstinat compeir not to offer his Repentance, then shall the Minister proceid, and say:—

Brethren, seing that as ye have heard this obstinate and impenitent persone, N., hath so grevously offended against God, and against this his holy congregatioun, who by no means (as ye may perceave) can be broght to repentance; whereof it is evident by the word of God, that he is fallin from the kingdome of heaven, and from the blessed society of the Lord Jesus:

And we, albeit with dolour of our hartes, may now execute that which the commandement of Jesus Christ, and the practise of his Apostle, schaweth that of our office we aucht to do, to wit, that we shall publictly declair and pronunce such to have no society with us, as declair themselfis obstinat and rebellious agains all holsome admonitions, and the blessed ordinances of his Church: and that we may dò the same, not out of our awin authority, bot in the name and power of our Lord Jesus Christ, befoir whom all kneis are compelled to bow, let us humblie fall down befoir him, and on this maner pray, and pronunce this sentence:—

The Invocatioun of the Name of Jesus Christ, to excommunicat the impenitent, togither with the Sentence of Excommunication.

O Lord Jesus Christ, the only and eternall King of all the chosen children of thine heavinly Father, the Head and Lawgiver of thy Church, who by thy awin mouth hast commanded that such offendars as proudlie contemne the admonitiouns of thy Church shall be cast out from the society of the same, and shall be reputed of thy professouris as prophane ethnicks; we, willing to

EXCOMMUNICATION.

obey this thy precept, which also we have receaved be institutioun of thy Apostile, ar here presently convened in thy Name, to Excommunicate and cast furth from the societie of thy holie bodie, and from all participatioun with thy Church in sacramentis or prayeris, N.; which thing we do at thy commandement, and in thy power and authoritie, to the glorie of thy holy Name, to the conservation and edification of this thy Church, in the which it hath pleised thee to place us Ministers, and to the extreme remedie of the stubburne obstinacie of the fore-named impenitent. And because thou hast promised thy self evir to be with us, bot especially with such as uprightly travel in the Ministery of thy Church, whom also thou hes promised to instruct and guyde by the dictament of thy Holie Spirit, we most humblie beseche thee so to governe and assist us in the execution of this our charge, that whatsoevir we in thy Name do here pronunce on earth, that thou wilt ratifie the same in the heavin. Our assurance, O Lord, is thy expressed word; and therefore, in boldnes of the same HEIR I, IN THY NAME, and at the commandement of this thy present Congregatioun, cut off, seclude, and excommunicat from thy body, and from our societie, N., as one persone sclanderous, proud, a contempnar, and one member, for this present, altogither corrupted and pernitious to the bodie. And this his sin (albeit with sorrow of hart) by vertew of our Ministerie, we bynde and pronunce the same to be bound in heaven and earth. We farther geve over in the handis and power of the Devill the said N., to the destructioun of his flesh, straitlie charging all that professe the Lord Jesus, to whose knawledge this our sentence shall cum, to repute and hald the said N. accursed, and unworthie of the familiar societie of Christians: declaring unto all men, that such as herefter befoir his repentance shall hant or familiarlie accompanie with him, ar partakaris of his impiety, and subject to the lyke condemnation. This our sentence, O Lord Jesus, pronunced in thy Name, and at thy commandement, we humblie desire thee to ratifie according to thy promise. And yit, Lord, thou that camest to save that which was lost, look upon him with the eyis of thy mercie, if thy good pleasure be; and so peirse thou his hart that he may feile in his breist the terrours of thy judgementis, that by thy grace he fruictfully may be converted to thee; and so damning his awin impietie, he may be with the lyke solemnitie receaved within the bosome of thy Church, from the which this day (with greif and dolour of our hartis) he is ejected.

LORD! in thy presence, we protest that our awin affections move us not to this severitie, but onely the hatred of sin, and obedience that we geve to thy awin commandement. And therefore, O heavenlie Father, we crave the perpetuall assistance of thy Holie Spirit, not onlie to brydill our corrupted affections, but also so to conduct us in all the course of our hole lyfe, that we nevir fal to the like impietie and contempt, bot that continuallie we may be subject to the voce of thy Church, and unto the Ministers of the same, who trewlie offer to us the Word of lyfe, the blessed Evangel of thy onlie belovit Sone Jesus Christ; to whom with thee and the Holie Spirit be all prayse, glorie, and honour, now and ever. So be it.

The Sentence pronunced, and the Prayer ended,

The Minister shall admonish the Church, that all the faithfull hald the Excommunicat as an ethnike, as before is said; that no man use his familiar companie; and yet that no man accuse him of onie uther cryme than of such as he is convicted of, and for the which he is excommunicat, bot that everie man shall secretlie call to God for grace to be granted to the excommunicat. Such as have office in the Ministerie may upon licence required of the Church, speik with the excommunicat, so long as hope resteth of his conversioun; bot if he contineu obstinat, then aucht all the faithfull utterly to abhor his presence and communication. And yit aucht they more earnestly to call to God that Sathan in the end may be confounded, and the creature of God fred from his snares by the power of the Lord Jesus. And with the accustomed benediction the Assemblie shall be dismissed, after they have sung the CI. Psalme, or one portion thereof, as it shall pleise the congregatioun.

The Ordoure to receave the Excommunicat agane to the Societie of the Church.

First, we must observe, that such as deserve death for the cryme committed, never be admitted to the Societie of the Church, untill such tyme as either the magistrate punish according to the law, or elles pardon the cryme, as before we have said: but such as for uther offences and for there contempt ar excommunicat, may be received when they shall earnestlie seike the favouris of the Church. They must begyne at the Ministerie, the Eldars, and Deaconis, who must expone there repentance to the Minister or Ministers in their Assemblie: a day may be appointed to the Excommunicat to present himself before them. The signes of his repentance aught to be diligentlie inquired, as what hath bene his behaviour sence the tyme of his excommunication, what he will offer for satisfaction to the Church, and unto whom he hath exponed the griefe and dolour of his hart. If the Excommunicat be found penitent and obedient in all things, the Minister the nixt Sonday may geve advertisement to the hole Church of his humiliation, and command them to call to God for increase of the same: the nixt session day the Minister may appoint to the Excommunicat such satisfaction as they think most expedient; to the which if the excommunicat fullie agree, then may the said Ministerie appoint

ABSOLUTION.

unto him a certane day when he shall fulfill the same.

For this is principallie to be observed, that no excommunicat persone may be receavid to the societie of the Church again, until such time as he hath stand at the church dure, at the least moe Sundayis than one; Which dayis being expirid, and the hole satisfaction complete, some of the Eldars shall passe to the excommunicat, efter that the formar prayer of the Minister in the pulpet be ended, and shall present him to an certan place appointed for the penitents, where he shall stand in the same habite, in the which he maid satisfaction, untill the sermon be ended: And then shal the same Eldars that broght him into the Church present him to the Minister, with these or the lyke wordis:

This creature of God is, N., that for his wickednes and obstinat rebellion hath bene Excommunicat from the bodie of Jesus Christ, bot now, by the power of the Spirit of God, is called back again by Repentance, so far as the judgement of man can persave, for he hath not only craved the favours of the Ministrie that he might be receaved into the bodie of the Church again, bot also most obediently hath subjected himself to all that we have commanded, for trial of his humiliatioun: And therefoir we present him befoir you to be examinat; and if his repentance be sufficient, to be receaved again to the bodie of the Church.

Then shall the Minister render thanks, first to God for that part of his humiliation, and also de-

sire the Church of God to do the same with him.
Therefter he shall addresse him to the person excommunicat, and first shall lay befoir him his sin; therefter, the admonitions that war gevin unto him to satisfie the Church for the same; and last, his proud contempt and long obstinacie, for the which he was excommunicat: And of every one he shall require his peculiar confession, with accusation of himself, and detestation of his impietie; Which being receaved, he shall render thanks to God as followeth:—

We thank the mercie and goodnes of God, through Jesus Christ our Lord, for this thy conversion, N., into the which thou hast not so much aschamed thy self, as that thou hast confounded and ovircome Sathan, by whose venoum and deceaveable entisements thou hitherto hast bene rebellious to the holsome admonitions of the Church: And yit because we can bot onlie see that which is externall, we will joyne our prayeris with thyne, that thy humiliation may proceed from the heart.

Let the Prayers appoynted to be said in the receaving of the Penitent [supra, *p. 54*] *be said also here: Which ended, let the Church and the Penitent be admonished as there is expremed: except that the cryme of his Excommunication must evir be aggredged and mentionat.*

ABSOLUTION. 79

The Prayer conteining his receaving to the Church.

Lord Jesus Christ, King, Teachar, and our eternal Preist, who with the preaching of thy blessed Evangel hes joyned the power to bynd and lowse the sinnes of men, who hes also pronunced, that whatsoevir by thy Ministers is bound on earth shall be bound in the heavin, and also that whatsoever is lowsed by the same, shall be lowsed and absolved with the in the heavin; look, O Lord, mercifullie upon this thy creature N., etc., whom Sathan of long tyme hath haldin in bondage, so that not onlie he drew him to iniquitie, bot also that he so hardened his hart, that he despised all admonitiouns; for the which his sin and contempt we war compelled to excommunicat him from our bodie. Bot now, O Lord, seeing that the Spirit of our Lord Jesus Christ hath so far prevaled in him, that he is returned to our society, it wil pleise thee, for the obedience of our Lord Jesus, so to accept him, that his formar inobedience be never laid to his charge, bot that he may increase in all godlines, till that Sathan finally be trodden under his feit and ours, by the power of our Lord Jesus Christ; to whom with Thee and the Holy Spirit be all honor and glorie, now and evir. So be it.

The Forme of Absolutioun.

In the Name and authoritie of Jesus Christ, I, the Minister of his blessed Evangel, with consent of this hole Ministery and Church, Absolve thee, N. from the sentence of Excommunication, from the sin by thee committed, and from al censures led againes thee for the same of before, according to thy repentance, and pronunces thy sin to be loused in heavin, and thee to be receaved again to the societie of Jesus Christ, to his bodie the Church, to the participatioun of his Sacramentes, and, finally, to the fruition of all his benefits, in the name of the Father, the Sone, and the Holy Spirit. So be it.

The Absolution pronounced, the Minister shall then call him Brother, and geve him admonition to watch and pray, that he fall not in the lyke tentation, that he be thankfull for the mercie shawin unto him, and that he shaw the fruictis of his conversion in lyfe and conversatioun.

Thereftir the hole Ministerie shall embrace him, and such utheris of the Church as be nixt unto him; and then shall a Psalme of thankisgeving be song.

This Ordour may be enlarged or contracted as the wisedome of the discreit Minister shall think expedient; For we rather shaw the way to the ignorant, than prescribe Ordour to the learned that cannot be amended.

Ane Prayer.

PRESERVE the publict face of thy Church, within this Realme, O Lord: Dilait the kingdome of thy Sone Jesus Christ universally; and so farther disclois and brek down the tyrannie of that Romane Antichrist, by the power of thy Sone our Lord Jesus Christ. So be it. ANNO 1567.

Rom. 16.—*Soli sapienti Deo per Jesum Christum gloria in perpetuum.* Amen.

> *This Book is thoght necessar and profitable for the Church, and commanded to be printed be the Generall Assemblie. Set furth be* JOHNE KNOX *Minister; and sighted be us whose names follow, as we war appointed be the said Generall Assemblie.*

JOHNE WILLOK.	DAVID LYNDESAY.
M. JOHNE CRAG.	GUILIELMUS CHRISTISONIS.
ROBERT PONT.	JAMES GREG, etc.
JOHNE ROW.	

The Visitation of the Sicke.

BECAWSE the Visitation of the Sicke is a thyng verie necessarie, and yet notwithstandyng, it is hard to prescribe all rules appertaynyng therunto, wee refer it to the discretion of the godlie and prudent Minister; who, accordinge as he seethe the pacient affected, either may lift hym up with the swete promesses of Godes mercy through Christe, if he perceive hym moche afrayde of Godes thretenynges; or contrarie wise, if he be not towched with the felinge of his synnes, may beate hym downe with Godes justice. Ever more like a skilfull phistion, framyng his medicine accordyng as the disease requireth; and if he perceyve hym to wante any necessaries, he not onelie releveth hym accordyng to his abilitie, but also provideth by others that he may be furnissed sufficiently. Moreover, the partie that is visited, may, at all tymes, for his comforte, sende for the Minister; who dothe not onelie make prayers for hym there presentlie, but also, if it so requyre, commendeth hym in the publique prayers to the Congregation.

A Prayer to be said in Visiting of the Sicke.

O OUR good God, Lord and Father, the Creator and conserver of all things, the fountaine of all

OF THE SICK. 83

goodnes and benignitie, like as (among other thine infinite benefites which thou of thy great goodnes and grace doest distribute ordinarly unto all men) thou givest them health of bodie, to the end that they shulde the better knowe thy great liberalitie, so that they might be the more ready to serve and glorifie thee with the same: So contrariwise, when we have il behaved ourselves in offending thy Majestie, thou hast accustomed to admonish us, and call us unto thee by divers and sundry chastisements, through the which it hath pleased thy goodnes to subdue and tame our fraile flesh: but especially by the grievous plagues of sicknes and diseases, using the same as a meane to awake and stirre up the great dulnes and negligence that is in us all, and advertising us of our evil life by such infirmities and dangers, especially when as they threaten the very death; which (as assured messingers of the same) are all to the flesh ful of extreme anguish and torments, although they be, notwithstanding, to the spirit of the elect as medicines bothe good and wholesome; for by them thou doest move us to returne unto thee for our salvation, and to cal upon thee in our afflictions, to have thine helpe, which art our deare and loving Father.

In consideration whereof, we most earnestly praye unto thee our good God, that it wolde please thine infinite goodnes to have pitie on this thy poore creature, whome thou hast, as it were, bound and tyed to the bed by most grievous sickenes, and brought to great extremitie by the heavines of thine hand.

O Lord! enter not into a compt with him, to render the rewarde due unto his workes; but throw thine infinite mercy remitte all his faultes, for the which thou hast chastised him so gently, and beholde rather the obedience which thy deare Sonne Jesus Christ our Lorde hath rendred unto thee; to wit, the sacrifice which it pleased thee to accept as a full recompense for all the iniquities of them that receive him for their justice and sanctification, yea, for their onelie Saviour.

Let it please thee, O God! to give him a true zeale and affection to receive and acknowledge him for his onlie Redeemer; to the end also that thou mayest receive this sicke person to thy mercie, qualifying al the troubles which his sinnes, the horror of death and dreadful feare of the same, may bring to his weake conscience. Neither suffer thou, O Lord, the assautes of the mightie adversarie to prevaile, or to take from him the comfortable hope of salvation, which thou givest to thy dearely beloved children.

And forasmuche as we are all subject to the like state and condition, and to be visited with like battel when it shal please thee to call us unto the same; we beseech thee most humbly, O Lord, with this thy poore creature whome thou now presently chastisest, that thou wilt not extend thy rigorous judgment against him, but that thou wouldest vouchsafe to shewe him thy mercie, for the love of thy deare Sonne, Jesus Christ our Lord: who, having suffered the moste shameful and extreame death of the crosse, bare willingly

OF THE SICK.

the faute of this poore patient, to the end that thou mightest acknowledge him as one redeemed with his precious blood, and received into the communion of his body, to be participant of eternal felicitie in the companie of thy blessed Angels. Wherefore, O Lord, dispose and move his heart to receave by thy grace, with all mekenes, this gentle and fatherlie correction which thou hast layed upon him; that he may indure it paciently, and with willing obedience, submitting himself with heart and minde to thy blessed wil and favourable mercie, wherein thou now visitest him after this sorte for his profit and salvation. It may please thy goodnes, O Lord! to assist him in all his anguishes and troubles: and although the tongue and voice be not able to execute their office in this behalf to set foorthe thy glorie, that yet at least thou wilt stirre up his heart to aspire unto thee onely, which art the onelie fountaine of goodnes; and that thou fast roote and settle in his heart the swete promises which thou hast made unto us, in Christ Jesus, thy Sonne our Saviour, to the intent he may remaine constant against all the assautes and tumultes which the enemie of our salvation may raise up to trouble his conscience.

And seing it hath pleased thee, that, by the death of thy dear Sonne, life eternal shuld be communicated unto us, and by the shedding of his blood the washing of our sinnes shulde be declared, and that by his Resurrection also, both justice and immortalitie shulde be given us; it may please thee to applie this holie and holesome medicine to this thy poore creature in such extremitie, taking from him all trembling and dreadful feare, and to give him a stoute courage in the middes of all his present adversiteis.

And forasmuche as all things, O heavenly Father, be knowen unto thee, and thou canst, according to thy good pleasure, minister unto him all suche things as shal be necessarie and expedient; let it please thee, O Lord, so to satisfie him by thy grace, as may seme most mete unto thy Divine Majestie.

Receive him, Lord, into thy protection, for he hath his recourse and accesse to thee alone; and make him constant and firme in thy commandements and promises: and also pardon all his sinnes, both secret and those which are manifest; by the which he hath moste grievously provoked thy wrath and severe judgements against him; so as in place of death (the which both he and all we have justly merited), thou wilt graunt unto him that blessed life, which we also attend and loke for by thy grace and mercie.

Nevertheles, O heavenly Father, if thy good pleasure be that he shal yet live longer in this worlde, it may then please thee to augment in him thy graces, so as the same may serve unto thy glorie: yea, Lord, to the intent he may conforme himself the more diligently, and with more carefulnes, to the example of thy Sonne Christ Jesus; and that in renouncing him self, he may cleave fully unto him, who, to give consolacion

OF THE SICK.

and hope unto all sinners, to obteine remission of all their sinnes and offences, hath caried with him into the heavens the theefe which was crucified with him upon the crosse.

But if the time by thee appoynted be come, that he shall departe from us unto thee, make him to feele in his conscience, O Lord, the frute and strength of thy grace; that thereby he may have a new taste of thy fatherlie care over him from the beginning of his life unto the very end of the same, for the love of thy deare Sonne Jesus Christ our Lord.

Give him thy grace, that with a good heart, and full assurance of faith, he may receive to his consolation so great and excellent a treasure: to wit, the remission of his sinnes in Christ Jesus thy Sonne, who now presenteth him to this poore persone in distres, by the vertue of thy promises reveiled unto him by thy worde, which he hath exercised with us in thy Church and congregation, and also in using the Sacraments, which thou therein hast established for confirmation of all their faith that trust in thee unfainedly.

Let true faith, O Lord, be unto him as a most sure buckler, thereby to avoyde the assautes of death, and more boldely walke for the advancement of eternal life; to the end that he, having a most livelie apprehension thereof, may rejoyce with thee in the heavens eternally.

Let him be under thy protection and governance, O heavenly Father; and although he be sicke, yet thou canst heale him; he is cast downe, but thou canst lift him up: he is sore troubled, but thou canst send redresse; he is weak, thou canst send strength, he acknowledgeth his uncleannes, his spots, his filthines, and iniquities, but thou canst wash him and make him cleane: he is wounded, but thou canst minister most sovereigne salves; he is fearful and trembling, but thou canst give him good courage and boldnes: To be short, he is, as it were utterly lost, and as a strayed shepe; but thou canst cal him home to thee againe. Wherefore, O Lord, seeing that this poore creature (thine owne workmanship) resigneth himself wholly into thy hands, receave him into thy merciful protection. Also we poore miserable creatures, which are, as it were, in the field, ready to fight till thou withdraw us from the same, vouchesafe to strengthen us by thine Holie Spirit, that we may obtaine the victorie in thy name against our deadlie and mortal enemie; and furthermore, that the affliction and the combat of this thy poore creature in most grievous torments, may move us to humble ourselves with all reverent feare and trembling under thy mightie hand, knowing that we must appeare before thy judgement seat, when it shal please thee so to appoint. But, O Lord, the corruption of our fraile nature is such, that we are utterly destitute of any meane to appeare before thee, except it please thee to make us suche as thou thy self requirest us to be; and further, that thou give us the spirit of meknes and humilitie, to rest and stay wholly on those things which thou onely commandest.

OF THE SICK.

But forasmuche as we be all together unworthy to enjoy such benefites, we beseche thee to receive us in the name of thy dear Sonne our Lord and Master, in whose death and satisfaction standeth wholy the hope of our salvation.

It may also please thee, O Father of comfort and consolation, to strengthen with thy grace those which imploy their travel and diligence to the ayding of this sicke persone, that they faint not by overmuch and continual labour, but rather to go heartilie and cherefully forwarde in doing their indevours towardes him: and if thou take him from them, then of thy goodnes to comfort them, so as they may paciently beare suche departing, and prayse thy Name in all things. Also, O heavenly Father, vouchesafe to have pitie on all other sicke persons, and such as be by any other wayes or means afflicted, and also on those who as yet are ignorant of thy trueth, and apperteine neverthelesse unto thy kingdome.

In like manner on those that suffer persecution, tormented in prisones, or otherwise troubled by the enemies of the veritie, for bearing testimonie to the same. Finally, on all the necessities of thy people, and upon all the ruins or decayes which Satan hath brought upon thy Church. O Father of mercy! spread forth thy goodnes upon all those that be thine; that we, forsaking our selves may be the more inflamed and confirmed, to rest onely upon thee alone. Graunt these our requestes, O our deare Father, for the love of thy deare Sonne our Saviour Jesus Christ; who liveth and reigneth with thee in unitie of the Holy Ghost, true God, for evermore. So be it.

Of Buryall.

THE corps is reverently brought to the grave, accompanied with the Congregation, without any further ceremonies: which being buryed, the Minister if he be present, and required, goeth to the Church, if it be not farre of, and maketh some comfortable exhortation to the people, touching death and resurrection.

The
Order of Public Worship.

When the Congregation is assembled at the houre appointed, the minister useth this confession following, or lyke in effect, exhorting the people dilligently to examin themselves, following in their hartes the tenor of his wordes.

The Confession of our Sinnes.

O ETERNALL God and moste mercifull Father, we confesse and acknowlage here, before thy divine majestie, that we are miserable synners, conceyved and borne in synne and iniquitie, so that in us there is no goodnes. For the fleshe evermore rebelleth against the spirite, wherby we contynually transgresse thy holy preceptes and commaundementes, and so purchase to our selves, through thy just judgement, death and damnation.

Notwithstandinge, O heavenly Father, forasmoche as we are displeased with our selves for the synnes that we have committed against thee, and do unfeynedly repent us of the same, we moste humbly beseche thee, for Jesus Christes sake, to shewe thy mercie upon us, to forgive us all our synnes, and to increase thy Holy Spirite in us. That we acknowlaginge from the bottome of our hartes our owne unrightousnes, may from hensforth not onely mortifie our sinfull lustes and affections, but also bringe forth suche fruites as may be agreable to thy moste blessed wyll; not for the worthynes therof, but for the merites of thy dearely beloved Sonne Jesus Christe, our onely Savyour, whom thou hast already given an oblation and offeringe for our synnes, and for whose sake we are certainly persuaded that thou wylt denye us nothinge that we shall aske in his name, accordinge to thy wyl. For thy Spirite doth assure our consciences that thou arte our mercifull Father, and so lovest us thy childrene through hym, that nothinge is able to remove thy heavenly grace and favor from us. To thee, therfore, O Father, with the Sonne and the Holy Ghoste, be all honor and glorye, worlde withowt ende. So be it.

An other Confession and Prayer

Commonly used in the Church of Edinburgh, on the day of commune prayers.

O DREADFUL and most mightie God, thou that from the beginning hast declared thyselfe a consuming fyre against the contemners of thy most holy preceptes; and yet to the penitent sinners hast alwayes shewed thy selfe a favourable Father, and a God full of mercie; We, thy creatures, and workmanship of thine owne handes, confesse our selves most unworthye to open our eyes unto the heavens, but farre lesse to appeare in thy presence. For our consciences accuse us, and our manifest iniquities have borne witnes against us, that we have declined from thee. We have bene polluted with idolatrie; we have given thy glorie to creatures; we have sought support where it was not to be founde, and have lightlyed thy most holesome admonitions. The manifest corruption of our lives in all estates, evidently proveth that we have not rightly regarded thy statutes, lawes, and holy ordinances; and this was not only done, O Lord, in the time of our blindnes, but even now, when of thy mercie thou hast opened unto us an entrance to thine heavenly kingdome by the preaching of thine holy Evangel, the whole body of this miserable Realme stil continueth in their former impietie. For the most parte, alas! following the footesteps of the blynde and obstinate Princesse, utterly despise the light of thyne Evangel, and delyte in ignorance and idolatrie; others lyve as a people without God, and without all feare of thy terrible judgementes. And some, O Lord, that in mouth professe thy blessed Evangel, by their sclanderous lyfe blaspheme the same. We are not ignorant, O Lord, that thou art a righteous Judge, that cannot suffer iniquitie long to be unpunished upon the obstinate transgressors; especially, O Lord, when that after so long blindnes and horrible defection from thee, so lovingly thou callest us again to thy favour and fellowship, and that yet we do obstinately rebel. We have, O

Lord, in our extreme miserie, called unto thee; yea, even when we appeared utterly to have beene consumed in the furie of our enemies, and then didest thou mercifully incline thine eares unto us. Thou foughtest for us even by thine owne power, when in us there was nether wisdome nor force. Thou alone brakest the yoake from our neckes, and set us at libertie, when we by our foolishnes had made our selves sclaves unto strangiers: and mercifully unto this day hast thou continued with us the light of thine Evangel, and so ceasest not to heape upon us benefites both spiritual and temporal. But yet, alas! O Lord, we clearly see that our great ingratitude craveth farther punishment at thy handes, the signes whereof are evident before our eyes. (.) For the whispering of sedition, the contempt of thy graces offered, and the mainteinance of idolatrie, are assured signes of thy farther plagues to fall upon us in particular for our greivous offences. And this unmeasurable untemperatnes of the ayre doeth also threaten thine accustomed plague of famine, which commonly followeth riotous excesse and contempt of the pore, wherewith, alas, the whole earth is replenished. (.) We have nothing, O Lord, that we may lay betwixt us and thy judgement but thyne only mercie, freely offred to us in thy deare Son, our Lord Jesus Christ, purchased to us by his death and passion. For if thou wilt enter in judgement with thy creatures, and keepe in minde our greivous synnes and offences, then can there no flesh escape condemnation. And,

therefore, we most humbly beseeche thee, O
Father of mercies, for Christ Jesus thy Sonnes
sake, to take from us these stony hearts, who so
long have heard aswell thy mercies as severe
judgements, and yet have not bene effectually
moved with the same; and give unto us hearts
mollified by thy Spirit, that may both conceive
and kepe in mynde the reverence that is due
unto thy Majestie. Looke, O Lord, unto thy
chosen children labouring under the imperfections
of the fleshe, and grant unto us that victorie that
thou hast promised unto us by Jesus Christ thy
Sonne, our onely Saviour, Mediator, and Lawgiver: To whome, with thee and the Holy Ghost,
be all honour and praise, now and ever.

A Confession of Sinnes,

To be used before Sermon.

TRUETH it is, O LORD, that we are unworthy to
come in thy godly presence, by reason of our manifold sinnes and wickednes, much lesse ar we worthie to receave any grace or mercy at thy handes,
if thou shulde deale with us according to our deservings; for we have sinned, O Lorde, against thee,
and we have offended thy godlye and divine
Majestie, if thou should beginne to reken with
us even from our first conception in our mothers
wombe, thou canst find nothing at al in us but
occasion of death and eternall condemnation: for
trueth it is, that first we are conceaved in sinne,

and in iniquitie was every one of us borne of oure mother; al the dayes of our lyfe we have so stil continued in sinne and wickednes, that rather we have geven oure selves to followe the corruption of this our fleshely nature then otherwaies, with that earnest care and diligence to serve and worship thee our God, as it become us; and therefore if thou should enter in judgement with us, just occasion hast thou not onely to punishe thir our wretched and mortal bodies, but also to punishe us bothe in bodie and soule eternally, if thou shoulde handle us according to the rigour of thy justice. Bot yet, O Lord, as on the owne part we acknowledge our owne sinnes and offences, together with the fearefull judgementes of thee our God, that justly be reason thereof thou may powre upon us, so also on the other parte we acknowledge thee to be a merciful God, a loving and a favourable Father to al them that unfainedly turne unto thee. Wherefore, O Lord, we thy people, and the workmanship of thine owne handes, most humbly beseche thee, for Christ thy Sonnes sake, to shewe thy mercy upon us, and forgive us al our offences, impute not to us the sinnes of oure youth, neither yet receave thou a rekening of us for the iniquitie of our olde age; but as thou hast showen thy self merciful to al them that hath truely called unto thee, so shew the like mercy and the lyke favour unto us thy poore servands. Indue our hearts, O God, with such a true and perfect acknowledging of our sinnes, that we may powre forth before thee the unfained sighs and sobbes of our troubled hearts and afflicted consciences for our offenses committed against thee. Inflamme our hearts with such a zeale and fervencie towardes thy glorie, that all the dayes of our lyfe our onely studie, travel, and labour may be to serve and worship thee our God in spirit, in trueth, and in veritie as thou requyrest of us ; and that this may be the better performed in us, preserve us from all impediments and stayes that in any waies may hinder or stop us in the same ; but in special, O Lord, preserve us from the craft of Satan, from the snares of the worlde, and from the noughtie lustes and affections of the fleshe. Make thy Spirit, O God, once to take such ful possession and dwelling in our hearts, that not onely al the actions of our life, but also al the wordes of our mouth, and the least thought and cogitation of oure mindes, may be gydit and rueled thereby. And, finally, graunt that al the time of oure lyfe may be so spent in thy true fear and obedience, that altogether we maye ende the same in the sanctification and honoring of thy blessed Name, through Jesus Christ our Lord ; to whome, with thee, and the Holy Ghost, be al honour and glorie for now and for ever. So be it.

A Confession of Sinnes, and Petitions,

Made unto God in the tyme of our extreame troubles, and yet commonly used in the Churches of Scotland, before the Sermon.

ETERNAL and everlasting God, Father of our Lord Jesus Christ, thou that showest mercy, and kepest covenant with them that love and in reverence kepe thy commandements, even when thou powrest foorth thy hote displeasure and just judgments upon the obstinat inobedient; we here prostrat our selves before the throne of thy Majestie, from our hearts confessing, that justelie thou hast punished us by the tyrannie of strangers, and that more justelie thou mayest bring upon us againe the bondage and yoak which of thy mercy for a season thou hast removed. Our kings, princes, and people in blindnes have refused the word of thyne eternall veritie; and in so doing, we have refused the league of thy mercy offered to us, in Jesus Christ thy Sonne, which albeit thou now of thy meere mercy hast offered to us againe in such aboundance, that none can be excused by reason of ignorance; yet not the lesse to the judgement of men, impietie overfloweth the whole face of this realme. For the great multitude delyte them selves in ignorance and idolatrie: and suche, alas! as appeare to reverence and embrace thy word, do not expresse the fruits of repentance, as it becometh the people, to whome thou hast showed thy selfe, so merciful and favourable. These are thy juste judgements, O Lord, whereby thou punishest sinne by sinne, and man by his owne iniquitie, so that there can be no end of sinne, except thou prevent us with thy undeserved grace. Convert us, therefore, O Lord, and we shall be converted; suffer not our unthankfulnes to procure of thy most just judgements, that strangers againe impire over us, neither yet that the light of thy Evangel be taken from us. But howsoever it be, that the great multitude be altogether rebellious, and also that in us there remaineth perpetual imperfections, yet for the glory of thine owne name, and for the glory of thine onely beloved Sonne Jesus Christ, whose veritie and Evangel thou of thy meere mercy hast manifested amongst us: it wil please thee to take us in to thy protection, and in thy defence, that all the worlde may know, that, as of thy meere mercy thou hast begone this worke of our salvation amongst us, so of this same mercy thou wilt continue it. Graunt us this, mercifull Father, for Christ Jesus thy Sonnes sake. So be it.

This done, the people singe a Psalme all together, in a playne tune; which ended, the Minister prayeth for th'assistance of God's Holy Spirite, as the same shall move his harte, and so procedeth to the Sermon. Usinge after the Sermon this Prayer followinge, or suche lyke.

A Prayer for the Whole Estate of Christes Churche.

ALMIGHTIE God and moste mercifull Father, we humbly submit our selves, and fall downe before thy Majestie, besechinge thee frome the botome of our hartes, that this seede of thy worde, nowe sowen amongest us, may take suche depe roote, that neither the burninge heate of persecution cause it to wither, nether the thorny cares of this lyfe do choke it, but that as seede sowen in good grownde, it may bringe forth thirtie, sixtie, and an hundreth folde, as thy heavenly wisdome hathe appointed. And becawse we have nede continuallie to crave many thinges at thy handes, we humbly beseche thee, O heavenly Father, to graunt us thy Holy Spirite to directe our peticions, that they may procede frome suche a fervent minde as may be agreable to thy moste blessed wyll.

And seinge that our infirmitie is hable to do nothinge without thy helpe, and that thou arte not ignorant with how many and great temptations, we poore wretches are on every side inclosed and compassed, let thy strengthe, O Lord, susteyne our weaknes, that we beinge defended with the force of thy grace, may be savely preserved against all assaultes of Satan, who goeth abowte continually like a roaringe lyon, sekinge to devoure us. Encrease our faith, O mercifull Father, that we do not swarve at any tyme frome thy heavenly worde, but augment in us hope and love, with a carefull

PUBLIC WORSHIP.

kepinge of all thy commaundementes, that no hardnes of harte, no hypocrisie, no concupiscence of the eyes, nor intysementes of the worlde, do drawe us away frome thy obedience. And seinge we lyve nowe in these moste perillous tymes, let thy Fatherly providence defende us against the violence of all our enemies, which do every where pursue us; but chiefely againste the wicked rage and furious uproares of that Romyshe idoll, enemie to thy Christe.

Fordermore, forasmoche as by thy holy Apostle we be taught to make our prayers and supplications for all men, we praye not onely for our selves here present, but beseche thee also, to reduce all suche as be yet ignorant, from the miserable captivitie of blindnes and error, to the pure understandinge and knowlage of thy heavenly trueth, that we all, with one consent and unitie of myndes, may wourshippe thee our onely God and Saviour. And that all pastors, shepherds, and ministers, to whome thou hast committed the dispensation of thy holy Woord, and charge of thy chosen people, may both in their lyfe and doctrine be fownde faithfull, settinge onely before their eyes thy glorie; and that by theim, all poore shepe which wander and go astray, may be gathered and broght home to thy foulde.

Moreover, becawse the hartes of rulers are in thy hands, we beseche thee to direct and governe the hartes of all kinges, princes, and magistrates to whome thou haste committed the sworde; especially, O Lord, according to our bonden dutie, we beseche thee to mainteyne and increase the honorable estate of this citie, into whose defense we are receyved, the magistrates, the counsell, and all the whole bodye of this common weale: Let thy Fatherlye favor so preserve theym, and thy Holy Spirite so governe their hartes, that they may in suche sorte execute their office, that thy religion may be purely mainteyned, manners refourmed, and synne punished accordinge to the precise rule of thy holy Woord.

And for that we be all members of the mysticall body of Christ Jesus, we make our requestes unto thee, O heavenly Father, for all suche as are afflicted with any kinde of crosse or tribulation, as warre, plague, famine, sikenes, povertie, imprisonement, persecution, banishement, or any other kinde of thy roddes, whether it be calamitie of bodie, or vexation of mynde, that it wold please thee to gyve them pacience and constancie, tyll thou send them full deliverance of all their troubles. And as we be bownde to love and honor our parentes, kinsfolkes, friendes, and contrye, so we moste humbly beseche thee to shewe thy pitie upon our miserable contrie of England, which once, through thy mercie, was called to libertie, and now for their and our synnes, is broght unto moste vile slavery and Babylonicall bondage.

Roote owte from thence, O Lorde, all raveninge wolves, which to fyll their bellies destroie thy flocke. And shewe thy great mercies upon those our brethrene which are persecuted, cast in prison, and dayly condemned to deathe for the testimonie of thy trueth. And thogh they be utterly destitute of all man's ayde, yet let thy swete comfort never departe from them, but so inflame their hartes with thy Holy Spirite, that thei may boldely and chearefully abide suche tryall as thy godly wisdome shall appoint. So that at lenght, aswell by their deathe as by their life, the kingdome of thy deare Sonne Jesus Christ may increase and shyne through all the worlde. In whose name we make our humble peticions unto thee, as he hath taught us.

OUR Father which arte in heaven, &c.

ALMIGHTIE and ever lyvinge God, vouchsave, we beseche thee, to grant us perfite contynuance in thy lively faith, augmentinge the same in us dayly, tyll we growe to the full measure of our perfection in Christ, wherof we make our confession, sayinge,

I BELEVE in God, &c.

Then the people singe a Psalme, which ended, the Minister pronounceth one of these blessinges, and so the Congregation departeth.

THE Lord blesse you and save you; the Lord make his face shyne upon you, and be mercifull unto you; the Lord turn his countenance towardes you, and graunt you his peace.

THE grace of our Lord Jesus Christ, the love of

God, and communion of the Holie Ghoste, be with you all. So be it.

It shall not be necessarie for the Minister dayly to repete all these thinges before mentioned, but beginnynge with some maner of Confession, to procede to the Sermon ; which ended, he either useth the prayer for all Estates before mentioned, or els prayeth, as the Spirite of God shall move his harte, framinge the same accordinge to the tyme and matter which he hath intreated of. And yf there shalbe at any tyme any present plague, famine, pestilence, warre, or such like, which be evident tokens of God's wrath ; as it is our parte to acknowlage our synnes to be the occasion therof, so are we appointed by the Scriptures to give our selves to mournynge, fastinge, and prayer, as the meanes to turn awaye God's heavie displeasure. Therfore, it shalbe convenient that the Minister at suche tyme do not onely admonyshe the people therof, but also use some forme of prayer, accordinge as the present necessitie requireth, to the which he may appoint, by a common consent, some severall daye after the sermon, wekely to be observed.

These Prayers that followe are used in the French Church of Geneva. The first serveth for Sunday after the Sermon, and the other that followeth is said upon Wednesday, which is the day of Commune Prayer.

Another manner of Prayer after the Sermon.

ALMIGHTIE God and heavenlie Father, since thou hast promised to graunte our requests, which we shal make unto thee in the name of our Lord JESUS CHRIST, thy welbeloved Sonne; and we are also taught by him and his Apostles to assemble our selves in his Name, promising that he wil be among us, and make intercession for us unto thee for the obteining of all such things as we shal agre upon here in earth; we, therefore, (having first thy commandement to praye for such as thou hast appoynted rulers and governours over us, and also for all things nedeful both for thy people, and for al sortes of men, forasmuche as our faith is grounded on thine holie worde and promises, and that we are here gathered together before thy face, and in the name of thy Sonne our Lord Jesus), we, I say, make our earnest supplication unto thee, our moste merciful God and bountiful Father, that for Jesus Christ's sake, our onelie Saviour and Mediator, it would please thee of thine infinite mercie, freely to pardon our offences, and in suche sorte to drawe and lift up our hearts and affections towardes thee, that our requestes may both procede of a fervent minde, and also be agreable unto thy most blessed wil and pleasure, which is onely to be accepted.

(.) We beseche thee, therefore, O heavenlie Father,

as touching all princes and rulers unto whome thou hast committed the administration of thy justice, and namely, as touching the excellent estate of the Quenes Majestie, and all her honorable Counsel, with the rest of the magistrates and commons of the realme, that it would please thee to graunte her thine holie Spirit, and increase the same from time to time in her, that she may with a pure faith acknowledge Jesus Christ thine onlie Sonne, our Lord, to be King of all kings, and Governour of all governours, even as thou hast given all power unto him both in heaven and in earth; and so give herselfe wholy to serve him, and to advance his kingdome in her dominions (ruling by thy worde her subjectes, which be thy creatures, and the shepe of thy pasture), that we being mainteined in peace and tranquillitie bothe here and everie where, may serve thee in all holines and vertue; and finally, being delivered from all feare of enemies, may render thankes unto thee all the dayes of our life.

We beseche thee also, moste deare Father and Saviour, for all suche as thou hast appoynted Ministers unto thy faithful people, and unto whome thou hast committed the charge of soules, and the ministerie of thine holie Gospel, that it would please thee so to guide them with thine holie Spirit, that they may be found faithful and zealous of thy glorie, directing alwaye their whole studies unto this end, that the poore shepe which be gone astray out of the flocke, may be soght

PUBLIC WORSHIP.

out, and broght againe unto the Lord Jesus, who is the chief Shepherd and head of all Bishops, to the intent they may from day to day grow and increase in him unto all righteousnesse and holines: And, on the other part, that it would please thee to deliver all the Churches from the daunger of ravening wolves, and from hirelings, who seke their owne ambicion and profit, and not the setting foorth of thy glorie onely, and the safegarde of thy flocke.

Moreover, we make our prayers unto thee, O Lord God, moste merciful Father, for all men in general, that as thou wilt be knowen to be the Saviour of all the worlde by the redempcion purchased by thine onely Sonne Jesus Christ; even so that such as have bene hitherto holden captive in darknes and ignorance for lacke of the knowledge of the Gospel, may, through the preaching thereof, and the cleare light of thine holy Spirit, be brought into the right way of salvation, which is to know that thou art onely very God, and that he, whome thou hast sent, is Jesus Christ: likewise, that they whome thou hast already endued with thy grace, and illuminated their hearts with the knowledge of thy worde, may continually increase in godlines, and be plenteously enriched with spiritual benefites; so that we may altogether worship thee, both with heart and mouthe, and render due honour and service unto Christ our Maister, King, and Lawmaker.

In like maner, O Lord of all true comfort, we

commend unto thee in our prayers, all such persones as thou hast visited and chastised by thy crosse and tribulation; all such people as thou hast punished with pestilence, warre, or famine; and all other persons afflicted with povertie, imprisonment, sicknes, banishment, or any like bodilie adversitie, or hast otherwise troubled and afflicted in spirit; that it would please thee to make them perceive thy fatherlie affection towarde them; that is, that these crosses be chastisings for their amendment, to the intent that they shulde unfainedly turne unto thee, and so by cleaving unto thee might receive ful comfort, and be delivered from all maner of evil. But especially, we commend unto thy Divine protection, all such which are under the tyrannie of Antichrist, and both lacke this foode of life, and have not libertie to call upon thy Name in open assemblie; chiefly, our poore brethren which are imprisoned and persecuted by the enemies of thy Gospel, that it would please thee, O Father of consolations, to strengthen them by the power of thine holie Spirit, in such sorte as they never shrinke backe, but that they may constantly persevere in thine holy vocation, and so to succour and assist them as thou knowest to be moste expedient, comforting them in their afflictions, mainteining them in thy safegarde against the rage of wolves, and increasing in them the gifts of thy Spirit, that they may glorifie thee their Lord God, both in their life and in their death.

Finally, O Lord God, most deare Father, we beseech thee to graunte unto us also, which are here gathered together in the name of thy Sonne Jesus to heare his worde preached, that we may acknowledge truely, and without hypocrisie, in how miserable a state of perdicion we are in by nature, and how worthely we procure unto our selves everlasting damnacion, heaping up from time to time, thy grievous punishmentes towarde us, through our wicked and sinful life, to the end, that (seing there remaineth no sparke of goodnes in our nature, and that there is nothing in us, as touching our first creation, and that which we receive of our parents, mete to enjoy the heritage of God's kingdome) we may wholly render up our selves with all our hearts, with an assured confidence unto thy dearly beloved Sonne, Jesus our Lord, our onely Saviour and Redeemer, to the intent, that he dwelling in us, may mortifie our olde man, that is to say, our sinfull affections, and that we may be renewed into a more godlie life, whereby thine holie Name (as it is worthy of all honour) may be advanced and magnified throughout the worlde, and in all places: likewise, that thou mayest have the tuicion and governance over us, and that we may learne dayly more and more to humble and submit our selves unto thy Majestie, in such sorte, that thou mayest be counted King and governour over all, guyding thy people with the sceptre of thy worde, and by the vertue of thine holie Spirite, to the confusion of thine enemies, through the might of thy trueth and righteousnes; so that by this meanes all power and height which withstandeth thy glorie, may be continually throwen downe and abolished, unto suche time, as the ful and perfect face of thy kingdome shal appeare, when thou shalt shewe thy selfe in judgement in the persone of thy Sonne; whereby also we, with the rest of thy creatures, may rendre unto thee perfect and true obedience, even as thine heavenly Angels do apply themselves and onely to the performing of thy commandements, so that thine onlie wil may be fulfilled without any contradiction, and that every man may bend him self to serve and please thee, renouncing their owne wiles, with all the affections and desires of the flesh. Graunt us also, good Lord, that we, thus walking in the love and dread of thine holie Name, may be nourished through thy goodness, and that we may receive at thine hands, all things expedient and necessarie for us, and so use thy gifte peaceably and quietly, to this end, that when we se that thou hast care of us, we may the more affectuously acknowledge thee to be our Father, loking for all good gifts at thine hand, and by with-drawing and pulling backe all our vaine confidence from creatures, may set it wholy upon thee, and so rest onely in thy moste bountiful mercie. And for so much as whiles we continue here in this transitorie life, we are so miserable, so fraile, and so much enclined unto sinne, that we fall continually and swarve from the right way of thy commandements, we beseech

PUBLIC WORSHIP.

thee pardon us our innumerable offences, whereby we are in danger of thy judgement and condemnation, and forgive us so freely, that death and sinne may hereafter have no title against us, neither lay unto our charge the wicked root of sin which doeth ever more remaine in us, but grant that by thy commandment we may forget the wrongs which other do unto us, and in steade of seking vengeance, may procure the wealth of our enemies. And for as much as of our selves, we are so weake, that we are not able to stand upright one minute of an houre, and also that we are so belaid and assalted evermore with suche a multitude of so dangerous enemies, that the devil, the worlde, sinne, and our owne concupiscences do never leave of to fight against us; let it be thy good pleasure to strengthen us with thy holie Spirit, and to arme us with thy grace, that thereby we may be able constantly to withstand all tentations, and to persevere in this spiritual battel against sinne, until suche time as we shal obteine the ful victorie, and so at length may triumphantly rejoyce in thy Kingdome, with our captaine and governour Jesus Christ our Lord.

This Prayer following, is used to be said after the Sermon, on the day which is appointed for commune Prayer: and it is very propre for our state and time, to move us to true repentance, and to turne backe God's sharpe roddes which yet threaten us.

Another Prayer.

God Almightie and heavenlie Father, we acknowledge in our consciences, and confesse, as the trueth is, that we are not worthie to lift up our eyes unto heaven, muche lesse mete to come into thy presence, and to be bolde to thinke that thou wilt heare our prayers, if thou have respect to that which is in us; for our consciences accuse us, and our owne sinnes doe beare witnes against us: yea, and we knowe that thou art a righteous Judge, which doest not counte sinners righteous, but punishest the fautes of such as transgresse thy commandements. Therefore, O Lord, when we consider our whole life, we are confounded in our owne hearts, and can not chuse but be beaten downe, and as it were despaire, even as though we were alreadie swallowed up in the depe goulfe of deathe. Notwithstanding, moste merciful Lord, since it hath pleased thee of thine infinite mercie, to commande us to call upon thee for helpe, even from the depe botome of hel; and that the more lacke and defaute we fele in our selves, so muche the rather we shulde have recourse unto thy soveraigne bountie; since also thou hast promised to heare and accept our requestes and supplications, without having any respect to our worthines, but onely in the Name, and for the merites of our Lord Jesus Christ, whome alone thou hast appointed to be our Intercessor and Advocate; we humble our selves

PUBLIC WORSHIP. 113

before thee, renouncing all vaine confidence in man's helpe, and cleave onely to thy mercie, and with ful confidence call upon thine holie name, to obtaine pardon for our sinnes.

First, O Lord, besides the innumerable benefites which thou doest universally bestowe upon all men in earth, thou hast given us such speciall graces, that it is not possible for us to rehearse them, no, nor sufficiently to conceive them in our mindes: As namely, it hath pleased thee to call us to the knowledge of thine holie Gospel, drawing us out of the miserable bondage of the Devill, whose sclaves we were, and delivering us from moste cursed idolatrie, and wicked superstition wherein we were plunged, to bring us into the light of thy trueth. Notwithstanding, such is our obstinacie and unkindnes, that not onely we forget those thy benefites which we have received at thy bountiful hand; but have gone astray from thee, and have turned our selves from thy law, to goe after our owne concupiscence and lustes, and neither have given worthy honor and due obedience to thine holie worde, neither have advanced thy glorie as our duetie required. And although thou hast not ceased continually to admonish us most faithfullie by thy Worde, yet we have not given eare to thy Fatherlie admonition.

Wherefore, O Lord, we have sinned and have grievouslie offended against thee, so that shame and confusion apperteineth unto us, and we acknowledge that we are altogether giltie before thy judgement, and that if thou wouldest intreat us according to our demerites, we could look for none other then death and everlasting damnation. For although we wolde go aboute to cleare and excuse our selves, yet our owne conscience wolde accuse us, and our wickednes wolde appeare before thee to condemne us. And in very dede, O Lord, we see by the corrections which thou hast alreadie used towardes us, that we have given thee great occasion to be displeased with us: for seing that thou art a just and upright Judge, it cannot be without cause that thou punishest thy people. Wherefore, for asmuche as we have felt thy stripes, we acknowledge that we have justly stirred up thy displeasure against us, yea, and yet we se thine hand lifted up to beate us afresh: for the roddes and weapons wherewith thou art accustomed to execute thy vengeance, are alreadie in thine hand; and the threatnings of thy wrath, which thou usest against the wicked sinners be in ful readines.

Now though thou shuldest punish us much more grievouslie then thou hast hitherto done, and that, whereas we have received one stripe, thou wouldest give us an hundreth: yea, if thou wouldest make the curses of thine Oulde Testament which came then upon thy people Israel, to fall upon us, we confesse that thou shouldest do therein very righteously, and we can not denie but we have fully deserved the same.

Yet Lord, for somuche as thou art our Father, and we be but earth and slyme; seing thou art our Maker, and we the workmanship of thine hands; since thou art our pastor, and we thy flocke; seing also that thou art our Redemer, and we are the people whom thou hast bought; finally, because thou art our God, and we thy chosen heritage, suffer not thine anger so to kindle against us, that thou shouldest punish us in thy wrath, neither remember our wickednes, to the end to take vengeance thereof, but rather chastise us gentlie according to thy mercie.

Trueth it is, O Lord, that our misdeeds have inflamed thy wrath against us, yet considering that we call upon thy Name, and beare thy marke and badge, mainteine rather the worke that thou hast begonne in us by thy free grace, to the ende that all the world may know that thou art our God and Saviour. Thou knowest that suche as be dead in grave, and whom thou hast destroyed and brought to confusion, will not set forthe thy praises; but the heavie soules, and comfortles, the humble hearts, the consciences opprest and loden with the grievous burthen of their sinnes, and therefore thyrst after thy grace, they shal set forthe thy glorie and praise.

Thy people of Israel oftentimes provoked thee to anger through their wickednes, whereupon thou didest, as right required, punish them; but so sone as they acknowledged their offences, and returned to thee, thou didst receave them alwaies to mercie: and were their enormities and sinnes never so grievous, yet for thy covenant's sake, which thou hadst made with thy servants Abraham, Isaak, and Jacob, thou hast alwaies withdrawne from them the roddes and curses which were prepared for them, in suche sort that thou didst never refuse to heare their prayers.

We have obteined by thy goodnes a farre more excellent covenant which we may alledge, that is, the covenant which thou first madest and stablishest by the hand of Jesus Christ our Saviour, and was also by thy divine providence written with his blood and sealed with his death and passion.

Therefore, O Lorde, we renouncing our selves, and all vaine confidence in man's helpe, have our only refuge to this thy most blessed covenant, whereby our Lord Jesus, through the offering up of his bodie in sacrifice, hath reconciled us unto thee. Beholde therefore, O Lorde, in the face of thy Christ, and not in us, that by his intercession thy wrath may be appeased, and that the bright beames of thy countenance may shine upon us to our great comfort and assured salvation: and from this time forwarde vouchsafe to receive us under thine holy tuicion, and governe us with thine holy Spirit, whereby we may be regenerat anew unto a farre better life:—

> So that thy Name may be sanctified: Thy Kingdome come: Thy Will be done in earth as it is in heaven: Give us this day our daily bread: And forgive us our detts even as we forgive our detters: And lead us not into tentation, but deliver us from evil: For thine is the Kingdome, and the power and the glorie for ever and ever. Amen.

PUBLIC WORSHIP.

And albeit we are most unworthie in our owne selves to open our mouthes and to intreat thee in our necessities, yet for as much as it hath pleased thee to commande us to pray one for another, we make our humble prayers unto thee for our poore brethren and membres whome thou doest visit and chastice with thy roddes and correction, moste instantly desiring thee to turne away thine anger from them. Remember, O Lord, we beseche thee, that they are thy children, as we are; and though they have offended thy Majestie, yet that it would please thee not to cease to procede in thine accustomed bountie and mercie, which thou hast promised shulde evermore continue towardes thine elect. Vouchsafe, therefore, good Lord, to extende thy pitie upon all thy Churches, and towardes all thy people, whome thou dost now chastise either with pestilence or warre, or such like thine accustomed roddes, whether it be by sicknes, prison, or povertie, or any other affliction of conscience and minde; that it wolde please thee to comfort them as thou knowest to be most expedient for them, so that thy roddes may be instructions for them to assure them of thy favour, and for their amendement, when thou shalt give them constancie and patience, and also aswage and stay thy corrections, and so at length by delivering them from all their troubles, give them most ample occasion to rejoyce in thy mercie, and to praise thyne holy Name: Chiefly that thou woldest, O Lord, have compassion aswel on all, as on everie one of them, that employ themselves

for the maintenance of thy trueth; strengthen
them, O Lord, with an invincible constancie, defend
them and assist them in all things and
everie where; overthrow the crafty practises and
conspiracies of their enemies and thyne; bridle
their rage, and let their bold enterprises, which
they undertake against thee and the membres of
thy Sonne, turne to their owne confusion; and
suffer not thy kingdome of Christians to be
utterly desolate, neither permit that the remembrance
of thine holy Name be cleane abolished in
earth, nor that they among whome it hath pleased
thee to have thy praises celebrated, be destroyed
and brought to nought, and that the Turkes,
Paganes, Papistes, and other infidels, might boast
themselves thereby, and blaspheme thy Name.

[*To this the Minister addeth that part which is
in the former prayer marked thus (.) page* 105.]

A Prayer used in the Churches of Scotland,

*In the time of their persecution by the Frenchmen:
but principally when the Lordes Table
was to be ministred.*

ETERNAL and everlyving God, Father of our Lord
Jesus Christ, we thy creatures, and the workmanship
of thine owne hands, sometymes dead by sinne,
and thral to Satan by meanes of the same, but
now of thy meere mercie called to libertie and
life by the preaching of thine Evangel, do take

upon us this boldnes (not of our selves, but of the commandement of thy deare Sonne our Lord Jesus Christ) to poure foorth before thee the peticions and complaints of our troubled hearts, oppressed with feare, and wounded with sorrowe. Trewe it is, O Lord, that we are not worthie to appeare in thy presence, by the reason of our manifold offences; neither yet are we worthie to obteine any comfort of thy hands, for any righteousnes that is in us. But seing, O Lord, that to turne backe from thee, and not to call for thy support in the time of our trouble, it is the entrance to death, and the plaine way to desperation; we therefore, confounded in our selves (as the people that on all sydes is assalted with sorrowes), do present our selves before thy Majestie as our soveraygne Capitane and onely Redemer, Jesus Christ, hath commanded us, in whose name and for whose obedience we humbly crave of thee remission of our former iniquities, aswel committed in matters of religion, as in our lyves and conversation. The examples of others that have called unto thee in their like necessities, give unto us esperance that thou wilt not reject us, neither yet suffer us for ever to be confounded. Thy people Israel did oftentymes declyne from thy lawes, and did follow the vanitie of superstition and idolatrie; and oftentimes didst thou correct and sharply punish them, but thou diddest never utterly despise them, when in their miseries unfainedly they turned unto thee. Thy Church of the Jewes were sinners, O Lord, and the most

part of the same did consent unto the death of
thy deare Sonne our Lord Jesus Christ; and
yet didst not thou despise their prayers, when in
the time of their grievous persecution they called
for thy support. O Lord, thou hast promised no
les to us, then thou hast performed to them, and
therefore take we boldness at thine owne commandement, and by the promise of our Lord
Jesus Christ, most humbly to crave of thee, that
as it hath pleased thy mercie partly to remove
our ignorance and blyndnes by the light of thy
blessed Evangel, that so it may please thee to
continue the same light with us, til that thou
deliver us from all calamitie and trouble. And
for this purpose, O Lord, it will please thee to
thrust out faithful workmen in this thy harvest
within this realme of Scotland, to the which,
after so long darcknes of Papistrie and superstition, thou hast offered the trueth of thine
Evangel in all purenes and simplicitie: continue
this thy grace with us, O Lord, and purge this
realme from all false teachers, from dumme dogs,
dissembled hypocrits, cruel wolves, and all
suche as shew themselves enemies to thy
true religion.

[*To this the Minister addeth that part which is
in the former prayer marked thus* (.) *page* 105.]

But now, O Lord, the dangers which appeare,
and the trouble which increaseth by the cruel
tyrannie of forsworn straingers, compelleth us to

complaine before the throne of thy mercy, and to crave of thee protection and defence against their most injust persecution. That nation, O Lord, for whose pleasure, and for defence of whome, we have offended thy Majestie, and violated our faith, oft breaking the leagues of unitie and concorde, which our kings and governours have contracted with our neighbours; that nation, O Lord, for whose aliance our fathers and predicessors have shead their blood, and we (whome now by tyrannie they oppresse) have oft susteined the hasard of battell; that nation finally, to whom, alwayes we have bene faithful, now after their long practised disceit, by manifest tyranny do seke our destruction. Worthely and justly mayst thou, O Lord, give us to be sclaves unto such tyrants, because for the mainteinance of their friendship we have not feared to breake our solemned othes made unto others, to the great dishonour of thyne holie Name; and therefore justly mayest thou punish us by the same nation, for whose pleasur we feared not to offende thy divine Majestie. In thy presence, O Lord, we lay for our selves no kynde of excuse; but for thy deare Sonne Jesus Christ's sake, we cry for mercie, pardon, and grace. Thou knowest, O Lord, that their craftie wittes in many things have abused our simplicitie; for under pretence of the maintenance of our libertie, they have sought and have found the way (unles thou alone confound their councels) to bring us in their perpetuall bondage. And now the rather, O Lord, do they seeke our destruction, because we have refused that Romane Antichrist, whose kingdome they defend in daily sheading the blood of thy Sainctes. In us, O Lord, there is no strength, no wisdome, no number nor judgement to withstand their force, their craft, their multitude and diligence; and therefore, looke thou upon us, O LORD, according to thy mercie. Beholde the tyrannie used against our poore brethren and sisters, and have thou respect to that despiteful blasphemie which uncessantly they spewe foorth against thyne eternal trueth ?

Thou hast assisted thy Church even from the beginning, and for the deliverance of the same thou hast plagued the cruel persecutors from tyme to tyme. Thy hand drowned Pharao; Thy sword devoured Amelec; Thy power repulsed the pride of Senacherib; And thyne angel so plagued Herod, that wormes and lice were punishers of his pryde. O Lord, thou remaynest one for ever; thy nature is unchangeable, thou canst not but hate crueltie, pride, oppression, and murther, which now the men whom we never offended, pretend against us: Yea further, by all meanes, they scke to banish from this realme, thy deare Sonne our Lord JESUS CHRIST: the true preaching of his worde, and faithful ministers of the same, and by tyranny they pretend to mainteine most abhominable idolatrie, and the pompe of that Romain Antichrist. Loke thou therefore upon us, O Lord, in the multitude of thy mercies: stretch out thine arme, and declare thy self protector of thy trueth: represse the pride, and daunten thou the furie of these cruell persecuters; suffer them never so to prevail against us, that the brightnes of thy word be extinguished in this realme; but whatsoever thou hast appoynted in thyne eternal counsel, to become of our bodies, yet, we most humbly beseche thee for Jesus Christ thy Sonnes sake, so to maintaine the puritie of thyne Evangel within this realme, that we and our posteritie may enjoy the fruition thereof, to the praise and glorie of thyne holie name, and to our everlasting comfort. And this we most affectuously desire of thy mercie, by the merites and intercession of our Lord Jesus Christ; to whom, with Thee and the Holie Ghost, be all honor, glory, prayse, and benediction, now and ever. So be it.

This is added so ofte as the Lord's Table is ministred.

Now last, O Lord, we that be here assembled to celebrate the Supper of thy deare Sonne our Lord Jesus Christ, who did not onely once offer his bodie and shead his blood upon the crosse, for our ful redemption, but also to kepe us in recent memorie of that his so great a benefite, provided that his bodie and blood shulde be given to us to the nourishment of our soules. We I say, that presently are convened to be partakers of that his most holy Table, most humblie do beseech thee to grant us grace, that in sinceritie of heart, in true faith, and with ardent and unfained zeale, we may receive of him so great a benefite: to wit, that frutefully we may possesse his bodie and his blood, yea Jesus Christ himselfe, very God and very man, who is that heavenly bread which giveth life unto the worlde. Give us grace, O Father, so to eate his flesh, and so to drink his blood that hereafter we live no more in our selves, and according to our corrupt nature, but that he may live in us, to conduct and guide us to that most blessed lyfe that abydeth for ever. Grant unto us, O heavenly Father, so to celebrate this day the blessed memorie of thy deare Sonne, that we may be assured of thy favour and grace towardes us. Let our faith be so exercised, that not onely we may seale the increase of the same; but also that the cleare confession thereof, with the good workes proceeding of it, may appeare before men to the praise and glory of thyne holie name, which are God everlasting, blessed for ever. So be it.

A Thanksgiving unto God

After our deliverance from the tyranny of the Frenchmen; with prayers made for the continuance of the peace betwixt the Realmes of England and Scotland.

Now, Lord, seing that we enjoye comfort both in bodie and spirite, by reason of this quiétnes of thy mercie graunted unto us, after our moste desperate troubles, in the which we appeared utterlie to have bene overwhelmed; we praise and glorifie thy mercie and goodnes, who piteously loked upon us when we in our owne selves were utterlie confounded. But seing, O Lord, that to receive benefites at thy hands, and not to be thankeful for the same, is nothing else but a seale against us in the day of judgement; we most humbly beseche thee to graunt unto us hearts so mindefull of the calamities past, that we continually may feare to provoke thy justice to punish us with the like or worse plagues. And seeing that when we by our owne power were altogether unable to have freed ourselves from the tyranny of strangers, and from the bondage and thraldome pretended against us, Thou of thyne especiall goodnes didst move the hearts of our neighbours (of whom we had deserved no such favour) to take upon them the common burthen with us, and for our deliverance not only to spend the lives of many, but also to hazarde the estate and tranquillity of their Realme and common wealth: Grant unto us, O Lord, that with such reverence we may remember thy benefites received, that after this in our defaute we never enter into hostilitie against the Realme and nation of England. Suffer us never, O Lord, to fall to that ingratitude and detestable unthankfulnes, that we should seke the destruction and death of those whom thou hast made instruments to deliver us from the tyranny of mercyles strangers. Dissipat thou the councels of such as deceitfully travel to stirre the hearts of the inhabitants of either Realme against the other. Let their malicious practises be their owne confusion: and graunt thou of thy mercy, that love, concorde, and tranquillitie may continue and encrease amongst the inhabitants of this yle, even to the comming of our Lord Jesus Christ, by whose glorious Evangel thou of thy mercie dost cal us both to unitie, peace, and Christian concord; the ful perfection whereof we shal possesse in the fulnes of thy Kingdome, when all offences shalbe removed, iniquitie shalbe suppressed, and thy chosen children be fully endued with that perfect glorie, in the which now our Lord Jesus reigneth: to whome, with Thee and the Holy Ghost, be all honour, praise, and glorie, now and ever. So be it.

A Prayer used in the Assemblies of the Church,

Aswel Particular as General.

ETERNAL and everliving God, Father of our Lord Jesus Christ, thou that of thyne infinite goodnes hast chosen to thy self a Church, unto the which ever from the fal of man thou hast manifested thy self: first, by thine owne voyce to Adam; next to Abraham and his sede, then to all Israel, by the publication of thy holy law; and last, by sending of thy onely Sonne, our Lord Jesus Christ, that great Angel of thy

Councel, into this worlde, and clad with our nature to teach unto us thy holie wil, and to put an end to all revelations and prophecies; who also elected to himselfe Apostles, to whom, after his Resurrection he gave commandement to publish and preache his Evangel to all realmes and nations; promising to be with them even to the end of the worlde; yea, and moreover, that wheresoever two or three were gathered together in his Name, that he wold be there in the midst of them, not onely to instruct and teache them, but also to ratifie and confirme suche things as they shal pronounce or decree by thy Worde.

Seing, O Lord, that this hath bene thy love and fatherly care towardes thy Church, that not onely thou plantedst it, rules and guydes the chosen in the same by thyne holy Spirite and blessed Worde; but also, that when the external face of the same is polluted, and the visible bodie falleth to corruption, then thou of thy mercies, providest that it may be purged and restored againe to the former puritie, aswel in doctrine as in maners: whereof thou hast given sufficient document from age to age; but especially now, O Lord, after this publike defection from thy trueth and blessed ordinance, which our Fathers and we have sene in that Romaine Antichrist, and in his usurped authoritie: Now (I meane) O Lord, thou hast reveiled thy selfe and thy beloved Sonne Jesus Christ, clearly to the world againe, by the true preaching of his blessed Evangel, which also of thy mercy is offered unto us within this Realme of Scotland; and of the same thy mercie hast made us Ministers, and burthened us with a charge within thy Church.

But, O Lord, when we consider the multitude of enemies, that oppone themselves unto thy trueth, the practises of Satan, and the power of those that resist thy kingdome, together with our owne weaknes, fewe nomber, and manifolde imperfections; we cannot but feare the sudden way-taking of this thy great benefite: and therefore, destitute of all worldely comfort, we have refuge to thine onely mercie and grace, most humbly beseching thee for Christ Jesus thy Sonnes sake, to oppone thine owne power to the pride of our enemies, who cease not to blaspheme thyne eternal trueth.

Give unto us, O Lord, that presentlie are assembled in thy Name, such aboundance of thy holy Spirit, that we may see those things that shall be expedient for the advancement of thy glory, in the midst of this perverse and stubburne generation. Give us grace, O Lord, that universally amongst our selves, we may agree in the unitie of true doctrine. Preserve us from damnable errors, and graunt unto us such puritie and cleaness of life that we be not sclanderous to thy blessed Evangel. Blesse thou so our weake labours, that the fruites of the same may redound to the praise of thy holy Name, to the profite of this present generation, and to the posteritie to come, through Jesus Christ our Lord; to whome, with Thee and the Holy Ghost, be all honor and praise, now and ever. So be it.

Ane Prayer, mete to be used when God threteneth his Judgements.

O LORDE our God, Father everlasting, and ful of compassion, heare from the heavens our prayers and supplications, which from our sorroweful hearts and wounded consciences we powre foorthe presently before thy Majestie. Thow hast, O Lord, in the multitude of thy mercies, not onely created us reasonable creatures, but also of thy inestimable goodnes hast send the great Angel of the covenant, our Lord Jesus Christ, to redeme us, by whome thy wrath is taken away, the law is satisfied, and the power of death, of hel, and of Sathan, is broken. Moreover, when as we lay in the shadowe of death, and the feareful darknes of the soule, which was brought in by that man of perdition the Antechrist, and his suppostes, conspired enemies to thy Sonne our Lord Jesus, thou made the light of thy Evangel to shyne amongst us in such aboundance, that no Nation nor Country hath the lamp of thy treuth, showing the way to life everlasting, so clerely shyning amongst them, with these benefits spiritual it pleaseth thee of the same goodnes to conjune temporal blessinges: for whose eyes hath not sene thy potent arme fighting for us, whose heart is so blinded that it can not perceave in al our afflictions thy wounderful delyverance: who can not but confesse that alwayes we were covered under thy shadow.

Thou was our hope, our fortresse, and our God, thou coverit us under thy winges, and we were sure under thy feathers. But alas, O Lord, the consideration of thy benefits is a matter of sorrow to our wounded consciences; for the multitude of thy blessings convicts us of the more feareful unthankfulnes. In suche a light what is among us but works of darknes; and so this thy great and inestimable kindnes, with unkindnes have we recompensed againe. Thou gently hast called us, and yet doest cal upon us, but who did heare? thou thretneth, but who did tremble? thow punisheth, but we wolde not receave correction. Ane fyre appeareth presently to be kendled in thy wrath, but where is the repentance amongst us to slocken it. O Lord, we know the dome, and insensible elements of the worlde admonisheth us, of our great unthankfulnes; the heavy face of the heavens, the unnatural dealings in the earth, the contagion and infection of the aire, thretneth thy judgements. Those creaturs thou has formed for mans comfort, but potent art thou who turneth that to the disconfort and hurt of them who repyneth against thee, which otherwise should have bene comfortabil. Besides al this things, we clerely see the enemies of thy trueth raging against thy Church to the judgement of man for to prevaile.

Yea, further, Lorde, Satan takinge upon him the shappe of an Angel of light, is in this corrupt

PUBLIC WORSHIP.

age moste besie, to shake the foundation of al trew religion; that he may involve againe the blind world in fearful darknes. Thir thy judgements, O thou righteous Judge of the world, ar hid from the eyes of them whome the God of this world hath darkned. But, O Lord, when we consider them, we must tremble; and when we behold them, we must stoupe and confesse that we have offended thy Majestie; O Lord, we dare not be bold altogether to crave that thou wilt not correct, for we understand that by external afflictions and corrections, as certeine middes and bitter medicine, thou hailest the woundes and sores of the inwarde man. Yet, Lord, correct us in thy mercy, and not in thy fearce wrath, lest peradventure we be brused into poudre; When as the fyre departeth from thy presence, and is kindled in thy indignation, seperate us from the nombre of those above whose headdes thy righteous judgements doeth hing, and the sword of thy vengeance thretneth eternal destruction; and to this end and purpose creat in us newe heartes, give unto us the sprite of unfained repentance, worke in us a sorrowing for our sinnes, a detestation and hatrent of the same, together with a love unto righteousnes, that we, not being conforme to the wicked world, but making thy reveled wil a rule to lead our lyfe by, may offer ourselves up in a lively sacrifice unto thee, consecrating unto thy glorie bodie and soule, and al the actions of the same. Preserve us, good Lord, from the fearful thraldome of conscience and bondage of idolatrie: continue the light of thy glorious Gospel amongst us: represse the pryde of them who seketh to have the kandlestick removed, and the light shyning extinguished. Purge this countrie, by suche means as thou knowest to serve best for thy owne glorie, of murther, fornication, adulterie, incest, oppression, sacrilege, and such like other pestes, which hath defyled thine inheritance. Graunt us thankful heartes for thy benefites and manifold blessings powred upon us, for the whiche also open our mouthes to sound thy praises and offer the sacrifice of thankesgeving wherein thou doste delyte; inarme us with thy power, to stryve against Satan, against the fleshe, against the worlde, and against al those thinges which driveth us away from thyne obedience, that walking in thy pathes, and obeying thy blessed ordinances, we may so end our lyves in the sanctification of thy Name, that at last we maye atteine to that blessed immortalitie, and that crowne of glorie prepared for thine elect in Jesus Christ the King of glorie and God of immortalitie; in whose Name we crave most humbly these thy graces to be powred upon us moste miserable sinners; and further, as thy wisedome knoweth to be necessary for us, and for thy Church universal, disparsed upon the face of the whole earth: praying unto thee with al humilitie and submission of mynds, as we ar teached and commanded to pray, saying: OUR FATHER which art, etc.

A Prayer in tyme of Affliction.

JUST and righteous art thou, O dreadful and most highe God, holy in al thy workes, and most just in al thy judgements, yea, even then when as thou punishest in greatest severitie. We have before, O Lord, felt thy heavy hand upon us, and when we cryed upon thee in our calamities and afflictions, moste mercifully thou inclyned thy ears unto us. But alas, O Lord, we have not answered in our lyves glorifying thy holy Name, as thou aunswered us when we called in oure distresse, but did returne unto our wounted sinne, and so provoketh thee through our misdedes unto displeasure: And therefore hast thou most justely turned thy self to punish us againe in bringing amongst us this noysome and destroying pest, according to the thretning of thy law, because we have not made our frute of thy former corrections. Our repentance, O Lord, hath bene like the dew that suddenly evanisheth away; yea, the great multitude abaide hardned in heart through their owne pryde, and, walking in the lusts of their owne hearts, securely contemned thy blessed ordinances. For who hath murned for the universal corruption of this blind age? or ceased the murtherer from his murther? the oppressour from his oppression? the deceatful man from his deceat? the contemner of thy word from his contempt? and the licentious liver from his licentiousnes? Yea, Lord, where could the man be found that soght not himself, albeit with the hurt of others and defacing of thy glorie? So universally did, and presently doeth, that root of al evil, covetousnes, ringe through out this whole cuntrie; yea, Lord, they to whome thou granted worldly blessings in greatest aboundance, hath bene and is possessed with this uncleane spirit of avarice. The more thou gave, the more insatiabilly thrysted they to have, and ceased not til they did spoyle thee of thy owne patrimonie; and yet in this matter they wil not knowe themselves to sinne and offend thy Majestie. Therefore can not thy Justice longer spare, but it must punishe and strike, as thou thretnest into thy holy Law. Now we know, Lord, that thy judgements commonly beginneth at thy owne house, and therefor hast thou begon for to correct us, albeit yet in thy mercie, and not in greatest severitie. Wherefore, good Lord, ether els in the multitude of thy mercies remove this bitter cuppe away from us, or graunt us thy grace paciently and obediently to drinke the same as geven out of thy owne hand for our amendement. We acknowledge, O Lord, that afflictions are molestsome, noysome, and hard to be borne with of fragil fleshe, but Christ Jesus hath suffered heaviar torments for us, and we have deserved more nor we susteine, who so oft hath merited the very hels. Yf it sal please thy Majestie to continew our punishement, and double our strypes, then lat it please thee in like means to eik our patience, and make oure corporal

PUBLIC WORSHIP. 135

afflictions serve to our humiliation, invocation of thy Name, and obedience to thy holy ordinances. Or if of a Fatherly pitie it shal please thee to be content with this gentle correction, let the calme appeare after this present tempest, that in respect of bothe the one and the other we may glorifie thee; in that first thou hast corrected to ammendement, lest we shuld have sleped in sinne to our destruction; and, secundly, that thou hast taken awaye the bitternes of affliction with the sweetnes of thy confortable deliverance: in thee first having respect to the necessitie, and in the laste to our infirmitie. But, Lord, againe we know albeit thy judgements thus beginneth at thy owne house, and they of thy familie appeareth only to be beaten of thee; yet the wicked shal not escape, but they shal drinke the dregges of the cup of thy indignation, let it be they escape the famine, the pest shal apprehend them; if they escape the pest, the sword shal devoure them; if they shal not fal in the edge of the sworde, thou art able to make any of the smallest and least creatures to be a stumblingblocke before their fete; where at, albeit they reche their heads above the clouds, they fal most fearefully. But, O Lord, now it is thine owne inheritance, for the which we sigh and grone before thy Majestie; loke upon it, therefore, from the heavens, and be merciful to thy people; let thy angre and thy wrathe be turned away from us, and make thy face to shine lovingly upon thine owne sanctuary. O Lord, heare; O Lord forgive; O Lord, consider, grant our requestes, for thy owne sake, O our God, and that in the Name of thy onely begotten Sonne Jesus Christ, our onely Saviour and Mediatour, in whose name we pray unto thee, as we are teached, saying, Our Father which art in heaven, hallowed be thy name : Thy Kingdome come : Thy Will be done in earth, as it is in heaven : Give us this day our daily bread : And forgive us our detts even as we forgive our detters : And lead us not into tentation, but deliver us from evil : For thine is the Kingdome, and the power, and the glorie, for ever and ever. Amen.

A Prayer for the Queen.

O LORD Jesus Christ, most high, most mightie King of kinges, Lord of lords, the onely Ruler of Princes, the very Sonne of God, on whose right hande sitting, doest from thy throne behald al the dwellers upon earth, with most lowly hearts we beseche thee, vouchesave with favourable regarde to behald oure most gracious sovereigne lord, King James the Sixte, and to replenish him with the grace of thy Holy Spirit, that he alway incline to thy wil and walke in thy way; kepe him farre of from ignorance, but through thy gift let prudence and knowledge alway abounde in his Royal heart; so instruct him (O Lord Jesus), ringing upon us in earth, that his humane Majestie alway obey thy Divine Majestie in feare and dreade: Indue him plentifully with heavenly gifts; graunt him in health and wealth long to live: Heap glorie and honour upon him: Glade him with the joye of thy countenance: So strengthen him, that he may vanquish and overcome al his and our foes, and be dread and feared of al the enemies of this his Realme.   Amen.

The
Maner of the Lordes Supper.

The day when the Lordes Supper is ministered, which Commonlye is used once a monthe, or so oft as the Congregation shall thinke expedient, the Minister useth to saye as followeth:

LET us marke, deare Bretherne, and consider how Jesus Christ did ordayne unto his Holy Supper, according as S. Paule maketh rehearsall in the 11. chapter of the First Epistle to the Corinthians:

"I have," saith he, "receyved of the Lorde that which I have delivered unto you, (to witt,) that the Lorde Jesus, the same night he was betrayed, toke breade, and when he had geven thankes, he brake it, sayinge, Take ye, eate ye, this is my bodie which is broken for you; doo you this in remembrance of me. Likewise after supper, he toke the cuppe, sayinge, This cuppe is the newe Testament or covenant in my bloude, doo ye this so ofte as ye shall drinke therof, in remembrance of me. For so ofte as you shal eate this bread and drinke of this cuppe, ye shall declare the Lordes deathe untill his comminge. Therfore, whosoever shall eate this bread, and drinke the cuppe of the Lorde unworthelye, he shalbe giltie of the bodye and bloud of the Lord. Then see that every man prove and trye hym selfe, and so let hym eate of this bread and drinke of this cuppe; for whosoever eateth or drinketh unworthelye, he eateth and drinketh his owne damnation, for not havinge due regarde and consideration of the Lordes bodye."

This done, the Minister proceadeth to exhortation.

DEARELY beloved in the Lorde, forasmoch as we be nowe assembled to celebrate the holy Communion of the body and bloud of our Saviour Christ, let us consider these woordes of S. Paule, how he exhorteth all persons diligently to trye and examine them selves before they presume to eate of that bread and drinke of that cuppe. For as the benefite ys great, if with a truly penitent hart and lively faith we receyve that holy sacrament, (for then we spiritually eate the fleshe of Christ and drinke his bloude, then we dwell in Christ and Christ in us, we be one with Christ and Christ with us,) so is the daunger great if we receyve the same unworthely, for then we be giltie of the bodye and bloud of Christ our Saviour, we eate and drinke our own damnation, not considering the Lordes bodye; we kindle Godes wrath against us, and provoke him to plague us with diverse diseases and sundry kindes of death.

And therefore, in the Name and authoritie of the eternal God, and of his sonne Jesus Christ, I excommunicate from this Table, all blasphemers of God, all idolaters, all murtherers, all adulterers, all that be in malice or envie, all disobedient persons to father or mother, princes or magistrates, pastors or preachers, all theves and disceivers of their neighbours; and finally, all suche as lyve a lyfe directly fighting against the wil of God: charging them as they wil aunswer in the presence of Him who is the righteous judge, that they presume not to prophane this most holy Table. And yet this I pronounce not to seclude any penitent person how grievous that ever his sinnes before have bene, so that he feele in his heart unfained repentance for the same; but only such as continue in sinne without repentance. Neither yet is this pronounced against suche as aspire to a greater perfection, then they can in this present life attayne unto.

For albeit we fele in ourselves much frailtie and wretchednes, as that we have not our faith so perfite and constant as we ought, being many tymes readye to distruste Godes goodness through our corrupt nature, and also that we are not so throughlye geven to serve God, neyther have so fervent a zeale to set forth his glory as our duetye requireth, felinge still such rebellion in our selves, that we have nede dayly to fight against the lustes of our fleshe; yet, nevertheles, seing that our Lorde hath dealed thus mercifully with us, that he hath printed his Gospell in our hartes, so that we are preserved from falling into desperation and misbeliefe; and seing also he hath indued us with a

THE LORD'S SUPPER. 141

will and desire to renownce and withstand our own affections, with a longing for his righteousenes and the keping of his commaundementes, we may be now right well assured, that those defautes and manifolde imperfections in us, shalbe no hinderance at all against us, to cause him not to accept and impute us as worthie to come to his spirituall Table. For the ende of our comming thyther is not to make protestation that we are upright and juste in our lives, but contrariwise, we come to seke our life and perfection in Jesus Christ, acknowledging in the meane tyme, that we of our selves be the children of wrath and damnation.

Let us consider, then, that this Sacrament is a singuler medicine for all poore sicke creatures, a comfortable helpe to weake soules, and that our Lord requireth no other worthines on our parte, but that we unfaynedly acknowlege our noghtines and imperfection. Then to the end that we may be worthy partakers of his merites and moste comfortable benefits, (which ys the true eatinge of his fleshe, and drinkinge of his bloud,) let us not suffer our mindes to wander aboute the consideration of these earthlie and corruptible thynges (which we see present to our eies, and fele with our handes,) to seeke Christ bodely presente in them, as if he were inclosed in the breade or wyne, or as yf these elementes were tourned and chaunged into the substaunce of his fleshe and blood. For the only waye to dispose our soules to receive norishment, reliefe, and quickening of his substance, is to lift up our mindes by fayth above all thinges worldlye and sensible, and therby to entre into heaven, that we may finde and receive Christ, where he dwelleth undoutedlye verie God and verie man, in the incomprehensible glorie of his Father, to whome be all praise, honor, and glory, now and ever. Amen.

> *The Exhortation ended, the Minister commeth doune from the pulpet, and sitteth at the Table, every man and woman in likewise takinge their place as occasion best serveth: then he taketh bread, and geveth thankes, either in these woordes followinge, or like in effect:*

O FATHER of mercye, and God of all consolation, seinge all creatures do knowlege and confesse thee as Gouverner and Lorde, it becommeth us, the workemanship of thyne own handes, at all tymes to reverence and magnifie thy Godly Majestie: first, for that thou haste created us to thyne own image and similitude; but chieflye that thou haste delivered us from that everlasting death and damnation, into the which Satan drewe mankinde by the meane of synne, from the bondage wherof, neither man nor angell was able to make us free; but thou, O Lord, riche in mercie and infinite in goodnes, haste provided our redemption to stande in thy onely and welbeloved Sone, whom of verie love thou didest give to be made man, lyke unto us in all thynges, (synne except) that in his bodye he myght receive the ponishmentes of our trans-

THE LORD'S SUPPER. 143

gression, by his death to make satisfaction to thy justice, and by his resurrection to destroye hym that was auctor of death; and so to reduce and bring agayne life to the world, frome which the whole offspringe of Adame moste justly was exiled.

O Lord, we acknowlege that no creature ys able to comprehende the length and breadthe, the depenes and height, of that thy most excellent love, which moved thee to shewe mercie where none was deserved; to promise and give life where death had gotten victorie; to receve us into thy grace when we could do nothyng but rebell against thy justice. O Lord, the blynde dulnes of our corrupt nature will not suffer us sufficiently to waye these thy moste ample benefites; yet, nevertheles, at the commaundement of Jesus Christ our Lorde, we present our selves to this his Table, (which he hath left to be used in remembrance of his death untyll hys comming agayne,) to declare and witnes before the world that by him alone we have receved libertie and life; that by hym alone thou doest acknowledge us thy children and heires; that by hym alone we have entrance to the throne of thy grace; that by hym alone we are possessed in our spirituall kingedome, to eate and drinke at his Table; with whome we have our conversation presently in heaven; and by whome our bodies shalbe reysed up agayne frome the dust, and shalbe placed with him in that endles joye, which thow, O Father of mercye, hast prepared for thyne elect, before the foundation of the world was layde. And these moste inestimable benefites, we acknowlege and confesse to have receaved of thy free mercie and grace, by thy onely beloved Sonne Jesus Christ: for the which therefore, we thy Congregation, moved by thy Holy Sprite, render thee all thankes, prayse, and glorie, for ever and ever.

> *This done, the Minister breaketh the bread, and delivereth it to the people, who distribute and divide the same among themselves, according to our Saviour Christ's commandement, and likewise giveth the cuppe. During the which time, some place of the Scriptures is read, which doeth lively set foorth the death of Christ, to the intent that our eyes and senses may not onely be occupied in these outwarde signes of bread and wyne, which are called the visible word; but that our hearts and mindes also may be fully fixed in the contemplation of the Lord's death, which is by this holie Sacrament represented. And after the action is done, he giveth thankes, saying:*

MOSTE merciful Father, we render to thee all praise, thankes and glorie, for that it hath pleased thee of thy great mercies to graunt unto us miserable sinners, so excellent a gift and treasure, as to receive us into the fellowship and companie of thy deare Sonne Jesus Christ our Lord, whome thou hast delivered to death for us, and hast given him unto us, as a necessarie foode and nourishment

THE LORD'S SUPPER. 145

unto everlasting life. And now we beseche thee also, O heavenly Father, to grant us this request, that thou never suffer us to become so unkinde as to forget so worthie benefites, but rather imprint and fasten them sure in our hearts, that we may growe and increase daily more and more in true faith, which continuallie is exercised in all manner of good workes; and so muche the rather, O Lord, confirme us in these perillous dayes and rages of Satan that we may constantlie stand and continue in the confession of the same, to the advancement of thy glorie, which art God over all things, blessed for ever. So be it.

The action thus ended, the people sing the 103 Psalme, "My soule, give laude," &c., or some other of thankesgiving: which ended, one of the blessings before mencioned, is recited, and so they rise from the table, and departe.

To the Reader.

If so be that any wolde mervel why we follow rather this Order, then any other in the Administration of this Sacrament, let him diligently consider, that first of all we utterly renounce the error of the Papistes: secondly, we restore unto the Sacrament his owne substance, and to Christ his propre place. And as for the wordes of the Lord's Supper, we rehearse them, not because they shulde change the substance of the bread or wine, or that the repetition thereof, with the intent of the sacrificer, shulde make the Sacrament (as the Papistes falsely beleeve) but they are red and pronounced, to teach us how to behave ourselves in that action, and that Christ might witnesse unto our faith, as it were with his own mouth, that he hath ordained these signes to our spirituall use and comfort: We do first therefore examine our selves, according to Saint Paules rule, and prepare our mindes, that we may be worthy partakers of so high mysteries. Then taking bread, we give thankes, breake and distribute it, as Christ our Saviour hath taught us. Finally, the ministration ended, we give thankes againe, according to his example: So that without his worde and warrant, there is nothing in this holie action attempted.

The
Forme of Mariage.

After the banes or contracte hathe byn publisshed thre severall dayes in the Congregation, (to the intent that if any person have intereste or title to either of the parties, they may have sufficient tyme to make theyr chalenge,) the parties assemble at the begynning of the sermon, and the Minister, at tyme convenient, saythe as followeth:

The Exhortation.

DEARLIE beloved Bretherne, we are here gathered together in the sight of God, and in the face of his Congregation, to knytt and joyne these parties together in the honorable estate of Matrimony, which was instituted and auctorised by God hym selff in Paradise, man beyng then in the state of innocencie. For what tyme God made heaven and earth, and all that is in theym, and had created and fasshoned man also after his owne similitude and likenes, unto whome he gave rule and lordship over all the beastes of the earth, fisshes of the sea, and fowles of the ayre; he said, It is not good that man lyve alone; let us make hym an helper like unto hym selff. And God brought a faste sleape uppon hym, and toke one of his ribbes and shaped Eva therof; doying us therby to understand, that man and wife are one body, one flesshe, and one blood. Signifyinge also unto us the mysticall union that is betwixt Christe and his Churche; for the which cawse man leaveth his father and mother and taketh hym to his wife, to kepe company with her; the which also he ought to love, even as owr Saviour loveth his Churche, that is to say, his electe and faithfull congregation, for the which he gave his liffe.

And semblably also, it is the wives dewtie to studie to please and obey her howsband, servyng hym in all thynges that be godlie and honeste; for she is in subjection, and under the governance of her howsband, so long as they contynew bothe alyve. And this holie mariage, beyng a thynge most honorable, is of suche vertew and force, that therby the howsband hathe no more right or power over his own bodie, but the wyfe; and likewyse the wyfe hathe no power over her own body, but the howsband; forasmoche as God hathe so knytt theym together in this mutuall societie to the procreation of children, that they should bryng theym up in the feare of the Lorde, and to the increase of Christes kyngdome.

Wherfore, they that be thus couppled together by God, can not be severed or put a parte, oneles it be for a season, with th'assent of bothe parties, to th'end to gyve theym selves the more ferventlie to fastyng and prayer; gyvyng diligent hede, in the meane tyme, that their longe beyng aparte be not a snare to bryng them into the daunger of

MARRIAGE.

Satan through incontinencie. And therfore to avoyde fornication, every man oughte to have his owne wyffe, and every woman her owne howsband: so that so many as can not lyve chaste, are bownde by the commandement of God to mary, that therby the holye temple of God, which is our bodies, may be kept pure and undefiled. For synce owr bodies are now become the very members of Jesus Christe, howe horrible and detestable a thyng is it to make theym the members of an harlot! Every one oght therfore to kepe his vessel in all purenes and holines; for whosoever polluteth and defileth the temple of God, hym will God destroye.

Here the Minister speakethe to the parties that shalbe mariede, in this wise:

I REQUIRE and charge you, as you will answer at the daye of judgement, when the secretes of all hartes shalbe disclosed, that if either of you do knowe any impediment whie ye may not be lawfully joyned together in matrimony, that ye confesse it; for be ye well assured, that so many as be coupled otherwise then Godes Woorde dothe allowe, are not joyned together by God; neyther is theyr matrimony lawfull.

If no impediment be knowen, then the Minister sayeth:

I TAKE you to wittenes that be here present, besechyng you all to have good remembraunce

150 THE FORM OF

hereof; and moreover, if there be any of you which knoweth that either of these parties be contracted to any other, or knoweth any other lawfull impediment, let theym nowe make declaration therof.

If no cause be alleaged, the Minister procedith, sayinge [To the Man]:

FORASMUCHE as no man speaketh agaynste this thynge, you, N., shall proteste here before God and his holy congregation, that you have takyn, and are now contented to have N., here present, for your lawfull wyfe and spowse; promisyng to kepe her, to love and intreate her in all thynges accordyng to the dewtie of a faythfull howsband, forsakyng all other durynge her lyfe; and briefelie, to lyve in a holy conversation with her, kepynge faythe and trewthe in all poyntes, according as the Worde of God and his holie Gospell dothe commaunde.

The Answere.

EVEN so I take her before God, and in presence of this his Congregation.

The Minister to the Spowse also sayethe:

YOU, N., shall proteste here before the face of God, in the presence of this holy congregation, that ye have takyn, and are now contented to have N., here present, for your lawfull howsband;

promisynge to hym subjection and obedience, forsakyng all other duryng hys lyfe; and fynallie, to lyve in a holy conversation with hym, kepinge faithe and truethe in all poyntes, as Godes Worde doth prescribe.

The Answere.

EVEN so I take hym before God, and in the presence of this his congregation.

The Minister then sayeth [*To the married couple*]:

GIVE diligent care to the [words of the] Gospell, that ye may understande how our Lorde wolde have this holy contracte kept and observed; and how sure and faste a knott it is, which may in no wyse be lowsed, accordyng as we be taughte in the 19. chapter of S. Mathewes Gospell :—

"The Pharisies came unto Christe to tempte hym and to grope his mynde, sayinge, Is it lawfull for a man to put away his wife for every lighte cawse? He answered, sayinge, Have ye not read, that He which created man at the begynnynge, made theym male and female? sayeng for this thyng shall man leave father and mother, and cleave unto his wife, and they twayne shalbe one flesshe; so that they are no more two, but are one flesshe. Lett no man therfore put asonder that which God hathe cowpled together."

If ye beleve assuredlie these woordes which owr Lorde and Saviour did speake, (accordyng as ye have hard them now rehearsed owte of the holy Gospell,) then may you be certayne, that God hathe evyn so knytt you together in this holy state of wedlocke. Wherfore applie your selves to lyve a chaste and holie lyfe together, in godlie love, in Christian peace, and good example; ever holdinge faste the band of charitie withowte any breache, kepinge faithe and trueth th'one to the other, even as Godes Woorde dothe appoynte.

Then the Minister commendeth theym to God, in this or suche like sorte :

THE Lorde sanctifie and blesse you; the Lorde powre the riches of his grace uppon you, that ye may please hym, and lyve together in holy love to youre lyves ende. So be it.

Then is songe the 128 Psalme, " Blessed are they that feare the Lorde," &c., or some other, appertaynyng to the same purpose.

The
Ordoure of Baptisme.

First note, that for asmoche as it is not permitted by God's Woord, that Wemen should preache or minister the Sacraments: And it is evident, that the Sacraments are not ordeined of God to be used in privat corners as charmes or sorceries, but left to the Congregation, and necessarely annexed to God's Woord as seales of the same: Therfore the infant which is to be baptised, shalbe broght to the churche, on the day appointed to comen prayer and preachinge, accompanied with the father and god-father. So that after the Sermon, the chyld beinge presented to the Minister, he demaundeth this question:

Do you present this childe to be baptised, earnestly desiring that he may be ingrafted in the mysticall body of Jesus Christ?

The Answer.

Yes, we require the same.

The Minister procedeth.

THEN let us consider, dearly beloved, how Almyghtie God hath not onely made us his children by adoption, and received us into the fellowship of his Churche; but also hath promised that he wilbe our God, and the God of our children, unto the thousand generation. Whych thinge, as he confirmed to his people of the Olde Testament by the sacrament of Circumcision, so hath he also renewed the same to us in his New Testament by the sacrament of Baptisme; doing us therby to wyt, that our infantes apperteyne to him by covenaunt, and therfore oght not to be defrauded of those holy signes and badges wherby his children are knowen from Infidells and Pagans.

Neither is it requisite, that all those that receyve this Sacramente have the use of understanding and faythe; but chiefelye that they be contayned under the name of God's people: So that remission of synnes in the bloode of Christ Jesus, doth appertaine to them by God's promise. Which thing is most evident by Sainct Paul, who pronounceth the children begotten and borne, either of the parents being faythful, to be cleane and holy. Also our Saviour Christ admitteth children to his presence, imbrasing and blessinge them. Which testimonies of the Holy Ghoste assure us, that infants be of the number of God's people; and that remission of synnes doth also apperteyne to theim in Christ. Therfore, wythout injurie, they cannot be debarred from the common signe of God's children. Neither yet is this owteward action of suche necessitie, that the lacke therof shuld be prejudiciall to their salvation, yf that prevented by death, thei may not

OF BAPTISM. 155

conveniently be presented to the church. But we (havinge respect to that obedience which Christians owe to the voice and ordinance of Christ Jesus, who commanded to preache and baptise all wythout exception,) do judge theym onely unworthy of any felowship with him, who contemptuosly refuse suche ordinary meanes as his wisdome hath appointed to the instruction of our dull senses.

Furthermore, it is evident that Baptisme was ordeined to be ministred in the element of water, to teache us, that lyke as water outwardly dothe washe away the fylthe of the bodye, so inwardly dothe the vertue of Christs's blood purge our sowles from that corruption and deadly poyson wherwith by nature we were infected. Whose venemous dreggs, althogh they continewe in this our flesh, yet by the merits of his deathe are not imputed unto us, by cause the justice of Jesus Christ is made ours by baptisme. Not that we thinke any suche vertue or power to be included in the visible water or owtward action, (for many have bene baptised, and yet never inwardly purged,) but that our Saviour Christ, who commanded baptisme to be ministred, will, by the power of his Holy Spirite, effectually worke in the harts of his elect (in tyme convenient) all that is ment and sygnified by the same. And this the Scripture calleth our regeneration, which standeth chiefli in these two points, in mortification, that is to say, a resisting of the rebellious lustes of the fleshe, and in newnes of lyffe, wherby we continually stryve to walke in that purenes and perfection wherwith we are cladd in Baptisme.

And althogh we in the journey of this lyffe be incumbred wyth many ennemies, which in the way assayle us, yet fyghte we not wyth out fruite. For this continuall battaill which we fight against synne, deathe, and hell, is a most infallible argument, that God the Father, mindfull of his promise made unto us in Christ Iesu, doth not only gyve us motions and courage to resist theim, but also assurance to overcome and obteine victorie.

Wherfore, dearly beloved, it is not only of necessitie that we be once baptised, but also it moch profiteth oft to be present at the ministration therof; that we beinge putt in minde of the league and covenant made betwxit God and us, that he wilbe our God, and we his people, he our Father, and we his children, may have occasion as wel. to trye our lives past as our present conversation, and to prove our selves, whether we stand fast in the faithe of God's elect, or contrariwise have strayed from him through incredulitie and ungodly lyvinge; wherof if our consciences do accuse us, yet by hearing the loving promises of our heavenly Father, (who calleth all men to mercie by repentance,) we may from hensforthe walke more warely in our vocation.

Moreover, ye that be fathers and mothers may take hereby moste singular comfort, to se your children thus receyved in to the bosome of Christes congregation, wherby you are daily admonished that ye norishe and bring up the children of God's favor and mercye, over whom his fatherly providence watcheth continually. Which thing, as it oght greatly to rejoyse you, (knowing that nothing can chaunce unto them wythout his good pleasure,) so oght it to make you diligent and carefull to nurture and instruct them in the true knowledge and feare of God. Wherin if you be negligent, ye do not only injurie to your own children, hydinge from them the good will and pleasure of Almyghtie God their Father, but also heape damnation upon your selves, in sufferinge his children, boght wyth the bloode of his deare Sonne, so trayterously (for lack of knowledge) to turn backe from him. Therfore it is your duety, with all diligence, to provide that your children, in tyme convenient, be instructed in all doctrine necessarie for a true Christian, chiefely that they be taught to rest upon the justice of Christ Jesus alone, and to abhorre and flee all superstition, Papistrie, and idolatrie. Finally, to the intent that we may be assured, that you the father and the suretie consent to the perfourmance hereof, declare here before God and the face of his congregation, the somme of that faith wherein you beleve, and will instruct this childe.

Then the Father (or in his absence the Godfather) shall rehearse the Articles of his Faith: which done, the Minister expoundeth the same as after followeth.

Ane Exposition of the Creed.

The Christian faith whereof now ye have briefly heard the somme, is commonly divided in twelve Articles: but that we may the better understand what is conteined in the same, we shal divide it into foure principal partes. The first shall concerne God the Father, The second, Jesus Christ our Lord. The third shal expresse to us our faith in the Holy Ghost. And the fourth and last, shal declare what is our faith concerning the Church, and of the graces of God freely given to the same.

First, of God we confesse three things, to wit, that he is our Father, Almightie, maker of heaven and earth. Our Father we call him, and so by faith beleve him to be, not so muche, because he hath created us (for that we have common with the rest of creatures, who yet are not called to that honour to have God to them a favourable Father;) but we call him Father, by reason of his free adoption, by the which he hath chosen us to lyf everlasting in Jesus Christ. And this his most singular mercie we preferre to all things, earthly and transitorie: for without this there is to mankind no felicitie, no comfort, nor finall joy; and having this we are assured that by the same love by the which he once hath freely chosen us, he shall conduct the whole course of our life, that in the end we shal possesse that immortall kingdome that he hath prepared for

OF BAPTISM.

his chosen children. For from this fountein of God's free mercie or adoption, springeth our vocation, our justification, our continual sanctification, and finally, our glorification: as witnesseth the Apostle.

The same God our Father we confesse Almightie, not only in respect of that he may do, but in consideration that by his power and godlye wysedome are all creatures in heaven and earth, and under the earth, ruled, guyded, and kept in that order that his eternal knowledge and wil hath appointed them.

And that is it which in the third part we do confesse that he is Creator of heaven and earth: that is to saye, that the heaven and the earth, and the contents thereof, are so in his hand, that there is nothing done without his knowledge, neither yet against his wil, but that he ruleth them so, that in the end his godly Name shalbe gloryfied in them. And so we confesse and beleeve, that nether the devils, nor yet the wicked of the world, have any power to molest or trouble the chosen children of God, but in so farre as it pleaseth him to use them as instruments, ether to prove and trye our faith and patience, or else to stirre us to more fervent invocation of his Name, and to continual meditation of that heavenly rest and joye that abideth us after these transitorye troubles. And yet shall not this excuse the wicked, because they never loke in their iniquitie to please God, nor yet to obey his wil.

In JESUS CHRIST we confesse two distinct and

perfect natures: to wit, the eternal Godhead and the perfect Manhood joyned together: so that we confesse and beleve, that that eternal Worde, which was from the begynning, and by the which all things were created, and yet are conserved and kept in their being, did, in the time appoynted in the counsel of his heavenly Father, receive our nature of a Virgine, by operation of the holie Ghost. So that in his conception, we acknowledge and beleve that there is nothing but puritie and sanctification; yea, even in somuche as he is become our brother. For it behoved him that shuld purge others from their sinnes, to be pure and clene from all spot of sinne, even from his conception. And as we confesse and beleve him conceived by the holy Ghost, so do we confesse and beleve him to be borne of a Virgine named Mary, of the tribe of Juda, and of the familie of David; that the promise of God and the prophecie might be fulfilled, to wit, "That the seede of the woman shulde breake downe the Serpent's head," and "that a Virgine shuld conceive and beare a childe, whose name shuld be Emmanuel, that is to say, God with us." The name Jesus, which signifieth a Saviour, was given unto him by the Angel, to assure us that it is he alone that saveth his people from their sinnes. He is called Christ, that is to say, Anoynted, by reason of the offices given unto him by God his Father; to wit, that he alone is appointed King, Priest, and Prophet. King, in that, that all power is given to him in heaven and earth; so

OF BAPTISM.

that there is none other but he in heaven nor earth, that hath just authority and power to make lawes to bynd the consciences of men; neither yet is there any other that may defend our soules from the bondage of sinne, nor yet our bodies from the tiranny of man. And this he doeth by the power of his worde, by the which he draweth us out of the bondage and sclavery of Satan, and maketh us to reigne over sinne; whils that we lyve and serve our God in righteousnesse and holynes of our life. A Priest, and that perpetual and everlasting, we confesse him, by reason that by the sacrifice of his own body, which he once offered up upon the crosse, he hath fullie satisfied the justice of his Father in our behalf: so that whosoever seketh any meanes besides his death and passion, in heaven or in earth, to reconcile unto them God's favour, they do not onely blaspheme, but also, so farre as in them is, renounce the fruit and efficacie of that his onely one sacrifice. We confesse him to be the onely Prophet, who hath reveiled unto us, the whole will of his Father in all things perteining to our salvation.

This our Lord Jesus we confesse to be the onlie Sonne of God, because there is none such by nature but he alone. We confesse him also our Lord, not only by reason we are his creatures, but chiefly because he hath redeemed us by his precious blood, and so hath gotten just dominion over us, as over the people whom he hath delivered from bondage of sinne, death, hel, and the devil, and hath made us Kings and Priests to God his Father.

We farther confesse and beleve, that the same our Lord Jesus was accused before an earthly judge, Pontius Pilate, under whome albeit oft and divers times he was pronounced to be innocent, he suffered the death of the crosse, hanged upon a tree betwixt two theves. Which death, as it was most cruel and vile before the eyes of men, so was it accursed by the mouth of God himselfe, saying, "Cursed is everie one that hangeth on a tree." And this kynde of death susteined he in our person, because he was appointed of God his Father to be our pledge, and he that shuld beare the punishment of our transgressions. And so we acknowledge and beleve that he hath taken away that curse and malediction that hanged on us by reason of sinne. He verely died, rendring up his spirit into the hands of his Father, after that he had said, "Father into thy hands I commend my spirit." After his death, we confesse his body was buryed, and that he descended to the hel. But because he was the Author of life, yea, the very lyfe itself, it was impossible that he shulde be retained under the dolors of death; and therefore the third day he rose agayn victor and conqueror of death and hel; by the which his resurrection, he hath brought life agayne into the world, which he by the power of his Holie Spirit, communicateth unto his lyvely membres; so that now unto them corporal death is no death, but an entrance into that blessed life, wherein

OF BAPTISM.

our head, Jesus Christ, is now entred. For after that he had sufficiently prooven his resurrection to his disciples, and unto suche as constantly did abide with him to the death, he visiblie ascended to the heavens, and was taken from the eyes of men, and placed at the right hand of God the Father Almightie, where presently he remaneth in his glory, onely Head, onely Mediator, and onely Advocate for all the members of his body: of which we have most especial comfort. First for that by his ascension the heavens are opened unto us, and an entrance made unto us, that boldly we may appeare before the throne of our Father's mercie. And, secondarylye, that we know that this honor and authoritie is given unto Jesus Christ, our head, in our name, and for our profite and utilitie. For albeit that in body he now be in the heaven, yet by the power of his Spirit he is present here with us, aswel to instruct us, as to comfort and mainteine us in all our troubles and adversiteis. From the which he shal finally deliver his whole Church, and every true member of the same, in that day when he shal visibly appeare agayn, Judge of the quicke and the dead.

For this finally we confesse of our Lord Jesus Christ, that as he was seene visibly to ascend, and so left the world, as touching that body that suffred and rose agayn; so do we constantly beleve that he shal come from the right hand of his Father, when all eyes shall see him; yea, even those that have pearced him; and then shall be gathered aswel those that then shal be found alive, as those that before have slept. Separation shalbe made betwixt the lambes and the goates; that is to say, betwixt the elect and the reprobate. The one shal heare this joyful voice, " Come ye the blessed of my Father, possesse the kingdome that is prepared for you before the beginning of the worlde." The other shal heare that feareful and irrevocable sentence, " Depart from me ye workers of iniquitie, to the fyre that never shalbe quenched." And for this cause, this day in the Scriptures is called " the day of refreshing," and " of the revelation of all secrets," because that then the just shall be delivered from all miseries, and shalbe possessed in the fulnes of their glory. Contrarywise, the reprobate shal receave judgement, and recompence of all their impietie, be it openly or secretly wrought.

As we constantly beleve in God the Father, and in Jesus Christ, as before is said; so do we assuredly beleve in the Holy Ghost, whome we confesse God equal with the Father and the Sonne; by whose working and mightie operation our darkenes is removed, our eyes spiritual are illuminated, our soules and consciences sprinkled with the blood of Jesus Christ, and we retayned in the trueth of God, even to our lyves end. And for these causes, we understand that this eternal Spirit proceding from the Father and the Sonne, hath in the Scriptures divers names. Sometymes called water, by reason of his pur-

OF BAPTISM.

gation, and giving strength to this our corrupt nature to bring foorth good fruite; without whome this our nature shuld utterly be barren, yea, it shuld utterly abound in all wickednes. Sometimes the same Spirit is called fyre, by reason of the illumination and burning heate of fyre that he kindleth in our hearts. The same Spirit also is called oyle, or unction, by reason that his working mollyfieth the hardnes of our hearts, and maketh us receive the print of that image of Jesus Christ, by whome onely we are sanctified.

We constantly beleve, that there is, was, and shalbe, even till the comming of the Lord Jesus, a Church, which is holy and universal; to wit, the Communion of Sainctes. This Church is holy, because it receaveth free remission of sinnes, and that by faith only in the blood of Jesus Christ. Secondly, because it being regenerat, it receiveth the Spirit of sanctification and power to walke in newnes of lyfe, and in good workes, which God hath prepared for his chosen to walk in. Not that we think the justice of this Church, or of any member of the same, ever was, is, or yet shal be so ful and perfect, that it nedeth not to stoupe under mercie; but that because the imperfections are pardoned, and the justice of Jesus Christ imputed unto such as by true faith cleave unto him. Which Church we cal Universal, because it consisteth and standeth of all tongues and nations; yea, of all estates and conditions of men and women, whome of his mercy God calleth from darknes to lyfe, and from the bondage and thraldome of synne to his spiritual service and puritie of life. Unto whome also he communicateth his Holy Spirit, giving unto them one faith, one head and soveraygne Lord, the Lord Jesus, one Baptisme and right use of Sacraments; whose hearts also he knitteth together in love and Christian concorde.

To this Church, holy and universal, we acknowledge and beleve three notable gifts to be graunted; to wit, remission of sinnes, which by true faith must be obteined in this lyfe. Resurrection of the flesh, which all shal have, albeit not in equal condition: for the reprobate (as before is sayd) shal rise but to fearful judgement and condemnation; and the just shal rise to be possessed in glory. And this resurrection shal not be an imagination, or that one body shal ryse for another; but every man shal receave in his owne bodie as he hath deserved, be it good or evel. The juste shal receave the life everlasting, which is the free gift of God given and purchased to his chosen by Jesus Christ, our onely Head and Mediator: to whome with the Father and the Holy Ghost be all honor and glory, now and ever.

Then followeth this Prayer.

ALMIGHTIE and everlasting God, which of thy infinite mercie and goodnes hast promised unto us that thow wilt not only be our God, but also

OF BAPTISM. 167

the God and Father of our children: we beseche thee, that as thou hast vouchesaved to call us to be partakers of this thy great mercie in the felowshipe of faithe, so it may please thee to sanctifie with thy Sprite, and to receive in to the number of thy children this infant, whom we shall baptise according to thy Woord, to the end that he comming to perfite age, may confesse thee only the true God, and whome thow hast sent Jesus Christ, and so serve him, and be profitable unto his churche in the whole course of his life; that after this life be ended, he may be broght as a lyvely member of his body unto the full fruition of thy joyes in the heavens, where thy Sonne our Christ raigneth, world wythout end. In whose name we pray as he hathe taught us:

Our Father, &c.

When they have prayed in this sort, the Minister requireth the child's name, which knowen, he saith:

N., I baptise thee in the name of the Father, of the Sonne, and of the Holy Ghoste.

And as he speaketh these words, he taketh water in his hand and layeth it upon the childes forehead: which done, he giveth thanckes as followeth:

FORASMOCHE, most holy and mercifull Father, as thow doest not only beawtifie and blesse us wyth common benefits, like unto the rest of mankinde, but also heapest upon us moste abundantly rare and wonderfull gyftes; of dutye we lyft up our eyes and mindes unto thee, and gyve thee most humble thankes for thy infinite goodnes, which haste not only nombred us emongest thy sainctes, but also of thy free mercie doest call our children unto thee, markinge theim wyth thys Sacrament as a singuler token and badge of thy love. Wherfore moste loving Father, thogh we be not able to deserve this so greate a benefite, (yea, if thow wouldest handle us according to our merits, we shuld suffer the punishement of eternall deathe and damnation,) yet for Christes sake we beseche thee, that thou wilt confirme this thy favor more and more towards us, and take this infant into thy tuition and defence, whom we offer and present unto thee wyth common supplications, and never suffer him to fall to such unkindes, wherby he shuld lose the force of this baptisme, but that he may perceyve thee continually to be his mercifull Father, throgh thy Holy Spirite working in his hart, by whose divine power he may so prevayle against Satan, that in the end, obteyning the victorie, he may be exalted into the libertie of thy kingdome. Amen.

The Ordoure

OF

The Generall Fast.

The Superintendentes, Ministers, and Commissioners of Kirkes reformed, within the realme of Scotland, convened in the Generall Assemblie, at Edinburgh, the 25 day of December 1565.

To all that trewly professe the Lord Jesus within the same realme, or els where, wishe grace and mercy from God the Father, and from his onely Sone our Lord Jesus Christ, with the perpetuall confort of the Holie Spirite.

THE present Troubles being somewhat considdered, but greater feared shortly to follow, it wes thought expedient (dearelie beloved in the Lord Jesus) that the whole Faithfull within this Realme shuld together and at one time, prostrat themselves before their God, craving of him pardone and mercy; for the great abuse of his former benefites, and the assistance of his Holy Spirite, by whose mightie operation we may yet so convert to our God, that we provoke him not to take from us the lyght of his Evangel, which he of his mercie hath caused so clearly of laite dayes to shine within this Realme.

But because that suche publicte Supplicationes

requyre alwayes Fasting to be joyned therewith, and publict Fastynge craveth a certane time, and certane exercises of godlynes then to be used with greater streatnes then at uther tymes; the whole Assemblie, after deliberation, hath appointed the last Sonday of February, and the first Sonday of Marche nixt following the date of the said Assemblie, to that moste necessare exercise (as tyme now standeth) of publict Fasting. And further, did require the same to be signified be all Ministers to their people the Sonday preceading the said last Sonday of Februarie.

But least that the Papistes shall think that now we begine to authorise and praise that which some tymes we have reproved and dampned in them; or els that the ignorant, who knowe not the commoditie of this moste godlie exercyse, shall contempne the same; we have thoght expedient some what to speak to the one and to the uther. And unto the Papistes, First, we say, that as in puritie of conscience we have refused their whole abhominationes, and, amongest the rest, that their supersticious and Pharisaicall maner of Fasting; so even unto this day do we continew in the same purpose, boldely affirming that their Fasting is no Fasting that ever God approved, but that it is a deceaving of the people, and a meare mocking of God, which moste evidentlie will appeare. If in the Scriptures we searche what is the ryght end of Fasting, what Fasting pleased God, and which it is that his soul abhorreth.

ON FASTING.

Of Fasting, in the Scriptures we finde two sortes; the one private, the other publicte. The private, is that which man or woman doeth in secrete, and before their God, for such causes as their owen conscience beareth record unto them. As David, during the time that his Sone, which wes begotten in adulterie, wes struken with mortall seicknes, fasted, weapt, and lay upon the ground, because that in the seicknes of the Chylde he did considder Godes displeasure against him self; for the removing whereof he fasted, murned, and prayed unto such tyme as he saw Godes wil fulfiled, by the awaytaking of the Chylde. Privatlie fasted Anna, wyfe to Alcana, even in the verray Solempne Feastes, during the time of hir barrennes; for she weapt and eat nothing, but in the bitternes of hir heart she prayed unto the Lord; nether ceased she from sorow and murning, unto suche tyme as Eli the hie priest concurred with her in prayers, by whose mouth, after that he had hard her petifull complaint, she receaved conforte.

Of this Fasting, speaketh oure Maister, Jesus Christ, in these words, " When ye fast, be not sowr as the Hypocrytes, for they disfigure their faces that they may seme unto men to fast; but thow, when thow fastest, anoynt thy heade and washe thy face, that thow seame not unto men to fast, but unto thy Father which seeth in secrete, and will rewarde thee opinly." Of the same no dout speaketh the Apostle, when that he sayeth

"Defraude not one another, except it be with consent for a tyme, that ye may give yourselves to Fasting and prayer."

To this private Fasting, which standeth chiefly in a temperat dyet, and in powring furthe of our secrete thoughtes and necessities before God, can be prescrived no certane rule, certane tyme, nor certane ceremonies; but as the Causes and occasiones why that exercise is used are divers (yea, so divers that seldome it is that many at ones are moved with one cause), so are diet, tyme, together with all uther circumstances, requyred to suche Fasting, put in the libertie of them that use it. To this Fasting we have bene faithfully and earnestly exhorted by oure Preachers, as oft as the Scriptures, which they entreated, offered unto them occasion. And we dout not but the godlie within this Realme have used the same as necessitie craved, albeit with the Papistes we blew no trumpets, to appoynt thereto certane dayes.

The uther kynde of Fasting is publict; so called, because that it is openlie avowed, some tymes of a Realme, some tymes of a multitude, some tymes of a cietie, and some tymes of a meaner company, yea, some tymes of particulare persones, and yet publictlie used, and that for the wealth of a multitude. The Causes thereof are also divers; for sometymes the feare of ennimies, some tymes the angrie face of God punishing, some tymes his threatning to distroy, some tymes iniquitie deprehended that ryghtlie before wes not.

ON FASTING.

considered, and some tymes the earnest zeale that some beare for preservation of Godes people, for advancing of his glorie, and performing of his worke according to his promes, move men to publicte Fasting, confession of their sinnes, and solempned prayers, for defence against their ennimies, recovering of Godes favoures, removing of his plagues, preservation of his people, and setting fordwarde of that worke, which he hath of his mercie promised to finishe, as in the subsequent probationes evidently shall appeare.

When Messingers came to Josaphat, saying, "There cometh a great multitude against thee, from beyond the sea, out of Aram (that is Syria), etc., Josaphat feared, and set him self to seke the Lord, and proclamed a Faste throughout all Juda. And Juda gathered them selves together, to aske counsall of the Lord; they come even out of all the cieties of Juda to inquyre of the Lord. And Josaphat stoode in the congregation of Juda and Jerusalem, in the hous of the Lord, before the new court; and all Juda stoode before the Lord with their yonge ones, their wyfes and their chyldrene. And Josaphat said, O Lord God of our fathers, are not thow God in heaven, and reignest not thow in all Kingdomes of the heathen? And in thy hand is power and myght, and none is able to withstand thee. Haste not thow, our God, cast out the inhabitantes of this land before thy people Israell, and haste given it to the sead of Abraham, thy freind, for ever? etc. But now the Ammorytes, and

Moabytes, and the Mont Seir, ar come to cast us
out of thy possession. O Lord our God, shall
thow not judge them? In us there is no strength
to stand against this great multitude that commeth
against us, nether knowe we what to do ; but
unto thee are our eyes bent, etc." Of this
Historie we have the first Cause of publict
Fasting, and the solempnitie thereof sufficientlie
prowen. For the feare of ennimies compelled
Josaphat to seik the Lord ; he knowing him selfe
burdened with the care of the people, exhorted
them to do the same. They fra all cieties and
quarters repared to Jerusalem, whereupone a
statute daye the King and the people, yea, wyves
and childrene, presented them selves before the
Lord, in his holy temple, exponed their necessitie,
implored his helpe against that enraged multitude,
that alwayes wes ennimie to Godes people, and
gave open confession of their owen weaknes, lean-
ing onely to the promes and protection of the
Omnipotent. Which exemple, we and everie
people likewyse assaulted, may and ought to
follow in everie poynt. This onely excepted, that
we are not bound to convene at any one appoynted
place, as they did at Jerusalem. For to no one
certane and severall place is that promes made,
that then wes made to the Temple at Jerusalem,
which wes, that whatsoever men in their extremitie shuld ask of God in it, God shuld grant
it from his holie habitation in the heaven. Jesus
the Messias, then looked for, whose presence wes
sought in the mercie seat, and betuix the Cheru-

binnes, is now entered within the vale, that is, in the heaven, and there abydeth onely Mediatorr of us, unto whome, from all the coastes of the earth, we may lift up pure handes, direct our prayers, supplicationes, and complaintes, and be assured that they shalbe receaved, in whatsoever place we convene. And, yet, in tyme of suche publict exercyses, we wolde wishe that all men and wemen shuld repare to suche places as their conscience may be best instructed, their Faith moste edified, repentance moste lively sturred up in them, and they by Godes worde may be moste assured that their just peticions shall not be repelled: Which thinges can not be done so lively in secrete and private meditation as that they are in publict Assemblie, where Christ Jesus is trewly preached: And this muche shortlie for the Firste head.

Of the Second, to wit, that the angrie face of God punishing aught to dryve us to publicte fasting, and humiliation of our soules before our God, we have two notable exemples, the one written in Josua; who, hearing and understanding that Israell had turned the back before the Cananites, and the elders of Israel rent their clothes, fell upone their faces before the Arke of the Lord unto the nyght, and caste dust upone their heades, in signe of their humiliation and dejection. The uther is expressed in the booke of the Judges, where Israell, being commanded by God to fight against Benjamin, because that they menteaned wicked men that deserved death, loste the first day twentie two thousand of their armie, and the second day eightene thousand. At the firste lose they were lyghtlie touched, and asked counsall if they shuld renew the battel; but at the second overthrow, the whole people repared unto the hous of the Lord, sat there, weapt before the Lord, and fasted that day unto the night; for then began they to considder Godes angrie face against them.

In this last historie there appeareth just cause why the people shulde have rune to the onely refuge of God, because that their first armie of fourtie thousand men wes utterlie distroyed. But what just occasion had Josua so lamentablie to complaine, yea, so boldely as it were to accuse God, that he had deceaved him in that, that against his promeis he had suffered Israell to fall before their ennimies. Wes the lose of thrette men (no mo fel that day in the edge of the sword) so great a mater, that he shuld despare of any better successe, that he shulde accuse God that he had brought them over Jordane, and that he shuld feare that the whole army of the Lord shuld be inveroned aboute, and consumed in the rage of their ennimies? Yea, if Israell had onely looked no further then to the lose of the fourty thousand men, they had bene but feable soldioures, for they had sufficient strength remaning behinde; for what were fourtie thousand, in respect of all the trybes of Israell?

Nay, nay, (deare Brethren) it wes an uther thing then the present lose, that terrified and effrayed their consciences, and made them so

ON FASTING.

effeminatlie (so wold fleshe judge) to complaine, weap, and owle before God; to wit, they saw his angrie face against them; they saw his hand fortifie their ennimies, and to fight against them, whome both he had commanded to fight, and had promised to give them victorie. For everie commandement of God to do any thing against his enniinies hath included within it a secrete promes of his godly assistance; which they fand not in the beginning of their interpryses; and therefore they did considder the fearcenes of his displeasure, and did tremble before his angrie face, whose myghtie hand they fand to fight against them; and that wes the cause of their dolorous complaintes, and fearfull crying before their God. What wes the cause that God delt so framedly with the one, and with the uther? We may perchance somewhat speak, when that we shall entreat of the frutes of Fasting, and of those thinges that may holde back from us the assistance of God, even when we prepare us to put his commandement in execution.

The Thride Cause of publict Fasting, is Godes threatninges pronounced, ether against a multitude, or against a persone in particulare. Of the former the exemple is Ninivie, unto the which Jonas cryed, Yet fourtie dayes, and Ninivie shalbe destroyed: which unpleasing tydinges cumming to the eares of the King, he proclamed a Faste, he humbled his owen soule, yea, even to sackcloth, and sitting in the duste, he straitlie commanded reformation of maners in all estates, yea, and that signes of repentance, of terroures, and feare, shuld appeare, not onely in men and wemen, but also in the brute beastes from whome wes all kynde of nurishement commanded to be withdrowen, to witnes that they feared aswell Godes judgementes to fall upone the creatures that served them in their impietie, as upone them selves that had provoked God to that hote displeasure. Of the uther the exemple is moste notable (moste notable we say) because that it fell in a wicked man, to wit, in Achab, who by instigation of his wicked wyfe Jesebell, saulde him self to do all iniquitie. And yet, when that he hard the fearefull threatninges of God pronounced by the Prophet Elias against him, against his wyfe and hous, he rent his royall garmentes, put on sackcloth, sleipt therein, fasted, and yead baire-footed. What ensewed the one and the uther of these, we shall after heare.

The Fourt Cause of publict Fasting and murning (for they two muste ever be joyned), is iniquitie deprehended, that before wes not ryghtly considered. The testimony whereof we have in Esdras, after the reduction of the captivitie, and that the temple and the work of the Lordes hous wes stayed. It wes shawen unto Esdras, that the people of Israell, the Preistes and the Levites, were not separat from the people of the nations, but that they did according to their abhominations; for they maryed unto them selves, and unto their sonnes, the doughters of the Cananites, the Pherisites, Hithetes, Jebusites, Ammorites

Moabites, and Egiptiens, so that the holy sead wes mixt with profane Idolateris: which thing being understand and more deaply considdered then it wes before, for then Esdras sawe just cause why the worke of the Lord prospered not in their handes. This considdered, we say Esdras taking upone him the sinne and offence of the whole people, rent his clothes, and pulled furth the heares of his head and beard, sat as a man desolate of all conforte till the evening Sacrifice; and then rysing, he bowed his kneis, and streached furth his hande before the Lord, and made a moste semple and humble confession of all the enormities that were committed be the people, aswell before the Captivitie as after their returning; and ceased not his lamentable complaint unto suche tyme as a great multitude of men, wemen, and childrene, moved by his exemple, weapt vehementlie, and promised redres of that present disordour and impietie.

Of the last Cause of publict Fasting, to wit, the zeale that certane persones beare for preservation of Godes people, for advancing of his glorie, and performing of his worke according to his promes: we have exemples in Mardocheus, Daniell, and in the faithfull assembled at Antioche. For when that Mardocheus herd of that cruell sentence, which, by the procurement of Haman, wes pronounced against his Nation; to wit, that upone a day, statute and affixed, shuld the Jewes, in all the provinces of the King Artaxarses, be destroyed, oulde and yong, men and wemen, and that their substance shuld be exponed in pray. This bloody sentence, we say, being herd, Mardocheus rent his clothes, put on Sackcloth and Ashes, past furth in the middest of the cietie, and cryed with a great and bitter crye; and, coming to the Kinges gate, gave knowledge to Ester what crueltie wes decreed against the Nation of the Jewes, willing her to make intercession to the king in the contrare, who, efter certane excuses, said, "Go and gather all the Jewes that are in Susan, and faste for me, eat not, nor drinke not, thre dayes and thre nyghtes; and I also, and my handmades, shall likewyse faste, and then shall I enter unto the King, although that I shuld perishe."

In this we may clearely se that the zeale that Mardocheus had to preserve the people of God, moved not onely him self to publict fasting, but also Ester, the Quene, her maides, and the whole Jewes that hard of the murther intended, and moved Ester also to hazart her lyfe in going unto the King without his commandement.

Of the uther, to wit, that the earnest desyre that God's servandes have that God will performe his promes, and manteane the worke that he hath begune, exemple we have in Daniell, and in the Actes of the Apostles. For Daniell, understanding the nomber of the yeares forespoken by the Prophet Jeremie, that Jerusalem shuld ly waist, to have bene completit in the first yeare of the reigne of Darius, turned him self unto God, fasted [humbled] him self in sackcloth and ashes,

ON FASTING.

and with unfeaned confession of his owen sinnes, and of the sinnes of the people, he vehementlie prayed, That according to the promises, some tymes made be Moyses, and after rehearsed by the prophet Isay and Jeremie, he wolde suddingly send them deliverance, and that he wolde not delay it for his owen Names sake.

When the Gentiles began to be illuminated, and that Anteochia had so boldely receaved the Evangle of Jesus Christ, that the disciples in it first of all tooke upone them the name of Christianes: The principall men of the same Church, thrusting no dout that the kingdome of Jesus Christ shulde further be enlarged, and that the multitude of the Gentiles shuld be instructed in the ryght way of salvation, fasted and prayed, and, whil that they wer so exercised, charge wes given that Paule and Barnabas shuld be seperated frome the rest, to the worke whereunto God had called them, etc.

Of these former Histories and Scriptures, we may clearely se for what causes publict Fasting and generale supplicationes have bene made in the Churche of God, and ought to be made when that ever the lyke necessities appeare, or occasions are offered. Now let us shortly heare what conforte and frute ensewed the same; for the ennimie, yea, the murtherar of all godly exercise is desperation; for with what courage can any man with continuance call upone God, if he shall disperatly dout whether God shall accept his prayer or not? How shall he humble him self before his throne, or to what end shall he confesse his offence, if he be not perswaded that there is mercy and good will in God to pardone his sinnes, to accept him in favour, and to grant unto him more then his owen heart, in the middest of his dolour can requyre or ymagine.

Trew it is, that this vennome of disperation is never throughlie purged from our heartes, so long as we cary this mortall carcasse. But yet the constant promises of our God, and the manyfolde documentes of his mercy and help, showen unto men in their greatest extremitie, ought to animat us to follow their exemple, and to hope for the same successe that they have gotten abufe mannes expectation. Josaphat, after his humiliation and prayer, obtened the victorie, with out the lose of any of his soldioures ; for the Lord reased Ammon and Moab against the inhabitantes of Mount Seir, who being utterly destroyed, everie one of the ennemies of God's people, lift his sworde against another, till that of that godles multitude, there was not one left alive. Josua and the Israelites after their dejection were conforted againe. Ninive was preserved, albeit that Jonas had cryed destruction. Yea, Achab, notwithstanding all his ungodlynes, lost not the frute of his humiliation, but wes recompensed with delay of the uttermoste of the plagues, during his lyfetyme. The murning of Esdras wes turned into joy, when that he saw the people willing to obey God, and the worke of the hous of the Lord to go fordwart. The bitter crying of Mardocheus, and the painefull

ON FASTING.

fasting of Ester, were aboundantly rewarded, when not onely wes the people of God preserved, but Haman their mortall enniemie wes hanged upon the same gallous that he had prepared for Mardocheus.

Daniell, after his fasting, confession, and prayer, gat moste notable revelationes and assurance, that his people shuld be delivered, yea, that in all extremities they shuld be preserved, till that the Messias promysed unto them shuld come, and manifestly showe him self. And the godly of Anteochea wer not frustrate of their conforte, when they herd how potently God had wrought amongest the Gentiles, by the ministerie of Barnabas and Paule. So that we may boldely conclude, that as God hath never despised the petitions of such as with unfeaned heartes have soght his comfort in their necessities, so will he not send us away emptie and voyd, if with trew repentance we seak his face.

If any wolde aske, In what extremitie we finde our selves now to be that heretofore we have not sene, and what are the occasiones that shuld move us now to humble our selves before our God by Publict Fasting, more then that we did in the beginning, when this Evangile wes now last offered unto us, for then, by all apperance, we and it in our persones stoode in greater danger, then we do yet? We answer, that the causes are mo then for greif of heart we can expresse. First, because that in the beginning we had not refused God's graces, but contrariwyse with such fervencie we receaved them, that we could beare with no kinde of impietie ; but for the suppressing of the same we nether had respect to frende, possession, land, or lyfe, but all we put in hasard that God's treuth myght be advansed, and idolatrie myght be suppressed. And, therefore did our God, by the mouth of his messingers, in all our adversities, assure us that our ennimies shuld not prevale against us, but that they shuld be subdewed under us, that our God shuld be glorified in our semple and upryght dealing. But now, sence that carnall wisdome hath perswaded us to beare with manifest idolatrie, and to suffer this Realme, which God hath once purged, to be polluted againe with that abhomination ; yea, alace, since that some of us, that God made sometymes instrumentes to suppresse that impietie, have bene the cheif men to conduct and convoy that Idole throughout all the quarters of this Realme ; yea, to the houses of them that sometymes detested the Masse, as the Devill and his service ; sence, that tyme, we say, we have found the face of our God angrie against us, his threatninges have bene sharpe in the mouthes of his Messingers ; which albeit for the tyme we dispysed and mocked, yet the just experience convicteth us that we were wicked, and that they in threatning us did nothing but the dewtie of God's trew Messingers.

And this is the Second cause that move us to this publict humiliation, rather now then in the beginning ; to wit, that then we followed God,

ON FASTING.

and not carnall wisedome, and therefore made he few in nomber fearefull to many, fooles before the world to confound the wyse, and such as before never had experience in armes, made God so bolde and so prosperous in all their interpryses, that the expertest souldioures feared the poore plowmen; yea, our God faught for us by sea and by land, he moved the heartes of strangers to supporte us, and to spend their lives for our releif. But now, alace, we se no signe of his former favour, for wisdome or manhead, strength and freindes, honour and blood, joyned with godlynes, are fallen before our eyes, to let us understand what shall be our destruction, if in time we turne not to our God, before that his wrathe be further kindled. But this is not the end: For esperance (or at least some opinion) had men before that God shulde move the Quenis Majesties heart, to heare the blissed Evangle of Jesus Christ truelie preached and so consequentlie that she shuld abandone all Idolatrie and fals Religion: But now she hath given answer in plaine wordes, that that Religion in which she hath bene nourished (and that is meare abhomination) she will manteane and defend. And in declaratioun thereof, of laite dayes, there is erected a displayed baner against Jesus Christ. For corrupted Hypocrites, and suche as have bene knowen deceavers of the people, are now authorized to spew out their vennome against Jesus Christ, his eternall trueth, and trew Messingers of the same. That Idole, the Masse, is now againe in divers places erected. And what hereof may ensew, yea, or what we may looke shalbe the end of suche unhappy beginninges, we desyre the godly deaply to considder.

But let it be granted that we had not fallen back from our former fervencie; that we saw not God's angrie face threatning us with more fearefull plagues to follow; that the best parte of our Nobilitie wer not exiled this Realme, neither yet that our Soverane were ennimie to our religion, that she beare no greater favour to flattering freres and to corrupted Papistes, then she doeth to our poore Preachers. Supponing, we say, that none of these foresaid causes we had to move us (as that we have them all, and mo, if that we list to recompt them), yet is there one, which if it move us not to humiliation, we showe our selves more then insensible. For now is Sathan so enraged against Jesus Christ, and so odius is the light of his Evangile unto that Romaine Antichrist, that to suppresse it in one province, Realme, or Nation, he thinketh it nothing, unles that in all Europe the godlie, and suche as abhorre the Papisticall impietie, be therewith also utterly distroyed, and so rased from the face of the earth, that no memorie of them shal after remaine.

If any think that suche crueltie cannot fall into the heartes of men, we send them to be resolved of those Fathers of the last Counsall of Trent, who, in one of their Sessions, have thus concluded: "All Lutheriens, Calvinistes, and suche as are of the new Religion, shall utterlie be exterminate. The beginning shalbe in France, by conducting of the Catholik kinge, Philip of Spaine and by some of the Nobilitie of France; which mater (say they) put to some stay, the whole force of bothe, together with the Pope's army, and force of the Dukes of Savoy and Farrar, shall assault Geneva, and shall not leave it till that they have put it to sack, saving in it no leving creature." And with the same mercie shal so many of France, as have taisted of the new religion be served. Frome thence expedition shalbe made against the Germaines, to reduce them to the obedience of the Apostolick seat. And so shall they procead to other Realmes and Nationes, never ceasing till that all be exterminate that will not make homage to that Romaine Idole. How fearefull a beginning this conclusion and determination had, France will remember mo ages then one: For how many, abufe a hundreth thousand men, wemen, babes, virgines, matrones, and aged fathers, suffered, some by sworde, some by water, some by fyre, and uther tormentes, the verray ennimies themselves are compelled to acknowledge. And albeit that God of his mercie in a parte disappoynted there cruell interpryses, yet let us not thinke that their will is changed, or their malice asswaged. No, let us be assured, that they abyde but oportunitie to finishe the worke, that cruellie against God, against his trueth, and the trew professoures of the same, they have begune. The whisperinges whereof are not secrete, neither yet the tokenes obscure, for the trafique of that dragone, now with the Princes of the earth, [and] his promyses and flattering entysementes, tend to none uther end, but to inflambe them against Jesus Christ, and against the trew professoures of his Evangle. For who can thinke that the Pope, Cardinalles, and horned Bishopes, will offer the greatest portion of their rentes, for susteaning of a warre whereof no commoditie shuld redound (as they suppose) to themselves? If any think that we accuse them without cause, let them heare their owen wordes; for this they wrate neare the end of the same Decree:

"And to the end that the holy Fathers on their parte, appeare not to be negligent or unwilling to give their ayde and supporte unto so holy a warre, or to spaire their owen rentes and money; have added, that the Cardinales shall content themselves of the yearely rent of five or six thousand ducates, and the rychest Bishope of two or three thousand at the moste; and to give franckly the rest of their revenues, to the intertenement of the warre, which is made for the extirpation of the Lutheriens and Calvinistes sect; and for reestablishing of the Romaine Churche, till suche tyme as the mater be conducted to a good and happy end."

If these be not open declarationes in what danger all faithful stand, if they can bring their crueltie to passe, let verray idiots judge. But let us heare their conclusion. "France and Germanie, (say they) being by these meanes so chas-

ON FASTING.

tised, abased, and conducted to the obedience of the holie Romaine Church, the Fathers dout not but tyme shall provide both counsal and commoditie, that the rest of the Realmes about may be reduced to one flok, and one Apostolick governour and Pastour," &c.

By this conclusion, we thinke that the verray blinde may see what is purposed against the Saintes of God in all Realmes and Nationes, to wit, destruction with crueltie, or els to make them to worship that blasphemous beast, who being an Idole, usurpeth to himselfe the name of universall Pastoure; and being knowen to be the Man of sinne and perdition, will be holden for an Apostolick governour. But some shall say, they are yet fare from the end of their purpose; and therefore we neid not to be so fearefull, nor so sollist. We answer, the danger may be nerar than we beleave, yea, perchance a parte of it hath bene neirar to our neckes, then we have considdered. But how so ever it be, seing that God of his mercie hath brought furth to lyght their cruell and bloody counsall, in which we nead not to dout, but still they continew; it becommeth us not to be negligent or sleuthfull; but we ought to follow the example of Ezechias, the King of Juda, who receaving not onely the dispytefull answere, but also the blasphemus and threatning letter of Sennaherib, first, send unto the Prophet Isayas, and pietifully compleaned of the instant troubles, willing him to make intercession unto God for the remanent that were left.

Unto whome, albeit that the Prophet answered comfortablie assuring the King, that the ennimie shuld not cume so neir as to shoote darte or arrow within Jerusalem; yet ceased not the godlie King to present himself in the Temple of the Lord; and as a man despared of all worldely conforte, spred abrod the letters that proud Sennaherib had sent unto him, and made unto God his moste fervent prayer, as in the 37 chapter of the Prophet Isayas we may read. The ennimie had turned backe, and God had put a brydle in his nosethirles. And so men myght have thought that the King neded not to have been so solliste. But the Spirite of God instructed the heart of his servand to seak helpe where it wes onely to be found, and from the handes of God, who only wes able to put finall end to that tyrannie. The exemple (we say) of this approved servand of God, we ought to follow now, when the like distruction is intended against us, yea, not against one Realme only, but against all that professe the Lord Jesus, as before we have heard. Albeit that God of his mercy hath stayed the furie of the Papistes for a tyme, we ought not to think that their malice is changed; nether that such as trewly professe the Lord Jesus, can be in securitie, so long as that Babyloniane hoore hath power to enchant the Princes of the earth. Let us therefore, understanding that she, being dronken with the blood of the Saintes, can never repent of crueltie and murther, use against her the spiritual weapones, to wit, earnest invocation of Gods Name, by the

ON FASTING.

which we finde the proude tyrannes of the earth, in tymes past, to have beene overthrowen.

Abufe all these Causes foresaid, we have yet one that ought not to be omitted, to wit, the body of this Realme hath long enjoyed quietnes, while that other nations about us have bene seveirly plagued. What thousandes dyed in the East Countreyes, and in England of the pest, Anno 1563, 1564; their own confessions beare record. What crueltie hath bene executed in France; what townes spoyled, and murther committed, somewhat before we have declared, and more we myght, if we had not respect to brevitie and tyme; and what trouble is presently, and long hath bene, betwix Denmarke and Swaden, the posteritie of that countrey will after understand. And in all this tyme, now sex yeares and more hath God spared us; so that the publict estate hath alwayes remaned quyet, except within these few monethes. Ought not the deap consideration of this move us now to stoupe before our God? For have we bene spared because that our rebellion to God is les then is the rebellion of those nations that we have sene punished? If so we think, we are far deceaved.

For in so great light of the Evangle, we thinke that greater inobedience wes never showen unto God, nor greater ingratitude unto his Messingers, sence the dayes of the Apostles, then of laite yeares hath bene (and yet is) within this Realme. Idolatrie is obstinatly menteaned; huredome and adulterie are but pastyme of the fleshe; slaughter and murther is esteamed small sinne, if any man have freind in Court: craftie dealing with the semple, disceat and oppression, is counted gude conques (yea, allace, almoste universally); parcialitie in judgement, is but interpretation of Lawes; yea delaying of Justice, what mater is that? What reverence is had to God's Messingers, and what respect unto the poore that now so multiplies within this Realme, (that the lyke hath seldome bene sene) thoght we will cease, the stones will crye, and condempne us: and yet what superfluitie, what vanitie, what feasting, ryotous banckating hath bene (and yet is) used in Court, countrey, and townes, althought the tounges of men dar not speak, yet we think the purses of some do feal, and in their maner complaine. If these be not sinnes that crave plagues from God, we humbly desyre men to consider what are the sinnes that were layed to the charge of Sodome and Gomorha by the Prophet Ezechiell.

Now, say we, God before our eyes hath punished uthers, and can he spare us, being more cryminall than they were? Nay, he can not. And, therefore, there restes nothing unto us but utter exterminion, if we unfeanedly turne not unto our God, before that his wraithe be further kindled against us. Judgement is begune in his owen Hous; for if within Scotland, amonges men of their estate, there wes to be fund equetie, justice, temperance, compassion upone the poore, and upryght conscience, they did moste clearely shyne in them whome God before oure eyes hath firste

ON FASTING.

dejected. Therefore yet agane we say, that onely repentance can save us from plagues more grevous then they have felt, or that we have sene of many yeares within this Realme.

But now we knowe, that suche as neither lufe God, nor trewly feare his judgementes (for mo Atheistes we have nor consumate Papistes within this Realme) shall grudge and crye, What new ceremonie is this that now we here of? Wherefore shall we Faste! and who hath power to command us so to do? A feg for their Fasting! we will fill and farse our bellies upone the oulde fassion, etc. Let not the godly be offended at the brocardes and lardons of such godless people; but let us tremble before our God, and considder that suche hath bene the proude contempt of the wicked in all ages before us, as in the Prophetes we may read. For Isay compleaneth, saying, "When the Lord calleth to sackclothe and ashes there is nothing heard but let us eat and drink, kill the fat, and make banket; let us bring wyne in aboundance, and more, and if we must dye, let us departe in joy; for so they ment, when that they said, Let us eat and drink, the morow we shall dye." But let us consider what answer they receave: "As I live, sayeth the Lord, this your iniquietie shall not be forgiven unto the death. I shall take from yow the myrth of wyne and oyle; your yong men shal fall by the sworde; your aged men shalbe led captives; your delicate dammes shall trote upon their fete over the river (meaning Euphrates); their buttockes shall be naked, and their shame shal not be hid," etc. Jeremie the Prophet preached and cryed even to the King and to the Quene, and commanded them to walke in lowlynes, to do justice, to represse impietie; and so he promised that they shoulde sit still upone their Throne in joy and quyetnes; but if they wolde not, he boldelie pronounced that their carcasses shalbe cast to the heit of the Sone, and to the frost and colde of the night. Ezechiel, in his age, useth the same ordour; and in his owen bodie showeth unto them signes of humiliation, and of the plagues that shuld apprehend them for their Rebellion.

All their admonitions were dispysed, we confesse; but thereto we shulde not looke, but unto that which ensewed suche proude contempt.

If we wolde that our palices shuld be so destroyed, that they shuld remaine desolate, and be dennes to dragones; if we wolde that our land shuld be laide waist, and be a pray to our enemies; and if we wolde that the rest of the plagues threatned by the Prophetes, and which have apprehended the disobedient before us, shuld come upone us in full perfection, then we nede nether to faste nor pray, repente nor turne to God: but and if we desyre ether to finde mercy in this lyfe, or joy and comfort in the lyfe to come, we muste showe ourselves unfeanedly sory for the abhominations that now universally Reigne; we must be lyke Lothe in Sodome, and Noah, in that Catholick defection from God, which wes into the first age; and by their exemples and notable deliverances ought we to be encoraged to showe our selves sory for this present corruption, and to oppone our selves thereto to the uttermoste of our powers, unles that we wolde have portion with the wicked.

Nether ought we to be discoraged because that the contemners, godles people, and mockers of all godlynes, shall prevale us in multitude. Their nomber, deare Brethren, shal not hurt our innocencie, if that we with unfeaned heartes turn unto our God; for the promes of his mercy is not bound unto the multitude, so that he will not heare but where the greatest parte is godly. No, deare Brethrene, wheresoever two or thre be gathered in his name, there is he in the middest of them; and againe, whosoever incalleth the name of the Lord, he shalbe saved, yea, even when in Godes displeasure the whole worlde shalbe plagued. And therefore let us not follow the multitude in evil doing; but let us declyne from the wayes of their vanitie, and by unfeaned humiliation of our selves, let us purches favoure, before that God's vengeance brust out lyke a fire.

THE power that we have to proclame this Fasting, is not of man, but of God, who, by the mouth of his Prophet Ezechiell, pronounceth this sentence: "If the watcheman se the sworde, or any other plague comming upone the land, if he blowe not the trumpet, and plainely warne them to turne to God, and if the sword come and take any away, the wicked shal perishe in their iniquitie; but their blood shalbe required from the handes of the watcheman." Now, so it is, that God of his mercy hath rased up amonges us mo watchemen then one or two, of whose mouthes we can not deny but we have hard fearefull threatninges of plagues to followe upone this proude contempt of all God's graces.

And therefore we, in the feare of our God, willing to avoyd the uttermoste of the plagues, have with one consent concluded this godly Exercise, to be used amonges us, in signe of our unfeaned humiliation; which albeit the godles shall mock, yet are we assured, that he who ones pronounced this sentence, "The soule that shall not be afflicted that same day, to wit, the day appointed to publict humiliation, shall perishe from amonges his people; yea, everie soule that shall do any worke that day, I shall destroye suche a soule frome the middest of his people." The ceremonie, and the certane statute day, we knowe to be abolished at the comming of Christ Jesus, together with the rest of the figurall ceremonies; but the effect thereof shall abyde so long as there abydeth an trew Church upon the face of the earth, unto the which repentance and remission of sinnes are publictly preached; and therefore, albeit we have no corporall punishment to inflict upone the contemners of that Godly exercise, yet have we the spiritual sword, which ones will stricke sorer then any materiall sword can or may.

The judgementes and justice of our God are immutable; he abydeth the same and one God that drowned the world by water; that consumed

Sodome and Gomorha with fyre from heaven; that plagued Pharo, destroyed Jerusalem, and hath executed his fearce judgementes in all ages, yea, and even before our eyes. It is the same God (we say) that this day by his faithfull servandes calleth us to repentance, whose voces if we contempne, we declare our selves Rebellious to our God, mockers of his threatninges, and suche as sometymes in despyte cryed, "We will walk according to the lust of our owen heartes, and let the counsal of the holy one of Israell cum as it list," etc. And if so we do, then wo, yea, wo and double damnation unto us, for then even as assuredly as God liveth, so assuredly shall the plagues that oure eares have oft heard, be poured furth upone us, even in the eyes of this same perverst generation, with whome we contempne God, and before whome we are nether feared nor eshamed stubburnlye to procead from sinne to contempt. Our hope is better of yow (deare Brethren) that have professed the Lord Jesus with us within this Realme, albeit that this we speake to let yow understand what Rebellion hath bene in flesh before us, and how it hath bene punished, that we may learne to stoupe before our God by unfeaned repentance; and then we shall be assured that, according to the promes made by the mouth of Joel, our God shal leave unto us a benediction, albeit that the vehement fyre of his wraith shall consume the inobedient.

But now, least that we shoulde thinke that the observation of the ceremonie is yneugh to please

God, we must understand what thinges must be joined with fructful Fasting, and what thinges they are that may make our Fasting odious to our God. And first we have to understand, that Fasting by it selfe considdered, is no suche thing as the Papistes heretofore have ymagined ; to wit, that it is a worke meritorious, and a satisfaction for the sinnes before committed. No, all they that faste with that intent, renounceth the merites of Christ's death and passion, in so farre as they ascrive to Fasting (whiche is but an exercise used by man) that whiche is onely proper to Jesus Christ ; which is, that he by offering up himself ones for all, hath made perfit for ever, those that shall be sanctified. We must further understand, that as the Kingdome of God is nether meat nor drink, so is nether Fasting by it selfe semple considdered, the cause why that Kingdome is granted to the chosen, nether yet eating (moderat we meane,) any cause why the reprobate are frustrat thereof. But unto Fasting there must be somewhat joyned, if that God shall looke upone it at any tyme in his favour. The Prophet Joel is witnes hereof, who in the persone of God, said unto suche as he had seveirly threatned. "Turne unto me in your whole heart, in fasting and murning." In which wordes the Holie Ghoste first requyreth the conversion of the heart unto God, and thereto joyneth fasting and murning, as witnesses of the sorow that we have for our former offences, and feare that we have of his seveir judgementes ; the releif whereof we publictly pro-

ON FASTING.

fesse we can obteane by no uther meanes, but by God's fre mercie from whome we have before declyned. So that the verray exercise of Fasting, and the murning, and prayer therewith annexed, do solempnedly protest, that by our Fasting, we merite not; for he that still confesseth his offence, and in bitternes of heart cryeth for mercy, doeth not brage of his merites. If the Papistes reply, Yet God looketh to the fasting, and heareth the prayers of suche as ryghtly humble themselves before him,—we deny not; but thereto we adde, that rightly did never man humble him self before God, that trusted or glorified in the merites of his owen workes; for without Faith it is unpossible to please God, and faith dependeth upone the promes of God's fre mercie through Jesus Christ, and not upone the merites of any workes. The Pharisie, in braging, wes rejected; but the Publican, in denying him self, and calling for mercie, wes justified, not by his workes, which he had not, but by grace and mercy, for the which he sobbed. Daniel fasted, confessed his sinnes, and the sinnes of the people, and thereto he added moste earnest and fervent prayers. But doeth he alledge any of them as a cause why God shuld ather be mercyfull to him or to the people, nay, we finde no suche thing, but the plaine contrarie, for thus he concludeth: "Now therefore our GOD, heare the supplication and prayer of thy servand, and showe thy pleasing visage unto thy Sanctuary, that lyeth waiste for the Lordes saik. O my God, give thy eare that thow mayest heare; and open thyen eyes, that thow maiste see the waist places of the cietie which beareth thy name: for we alledge not our ryghteousnes in our prayers, that we poure furthe before thee, but thy moste abounding mercy: Lord! heare; Lord! be mercyfull; Lord! take head, and helpe, and delay not, for thine owen self, my God!"

We may plainely se whereupon this excellent servand of God grounded himself to purches God's favour; to wit, upone the Lord, that is, upone the Saviour and Mediator promised, upone the moste aboundant mercie of God, and upone God himselfe; for he understoode what God had promised, aswell by the mouth of Moyses, as by the Prophet Isais, saying: "Beholde that I am, yea, even I am the Lord, and there is no GOD but I: I kill, and I give lyfe againe: I give the wound, and I shall heale: For my owen Names saike will I do it, sayeth the Eternall." Apone these and the lyke promises, we say, did all the Sainctes of God in all their extremities depend, and did looke to receave comforte, without all respect to their owen workes; they dampned the best of their owen workes, and called them nothing but filthiness before God. And therefore yet, as of before, we boldely affirme, that the Papisticall fasting wes not onlie vaine (for what fasting is it to absteane from fleshe, and to fill the bellie with fishe, wyne, spyce, and uther delicates?) but also it wes odious unto God, and blasphemous to the death of Jesus Christ, for the causes forewritten. And this

ON FASTING. 201

muche shortly for those thinges that must be joyned with frutefull Fasting.

Now we have to consider what thinges may make our Fasting odious, besydes this proude opinion of merite, whereof we have spoken.

It is no dout but that infidelitie maketh all the workes of the reprobate odious before God, yea, even when that they do the verray workes that God hath commanded, as we may read in Matt. 5. 6. and 7., Isai 1. and 66. etc., and divers uther places. But because that infidelitie lurketh oft in the heart, and can not well be espyed but by the bitter and rotten frutes that spring thereof, the Spirite of God hath painted furthe unto us in plaine wordes, what vices may make us and all our workes odious before our God, so that nether will he heare our prayers, nor regarde our fasting. Salomon sayeth, "He that ditteth his eare from the crye of the poore, his prayer shalbe abhominable before God." And Isai, in the persone of God, sayeth: "Albeit that ye shall stretche out your handes, and multiplie your prayers, yet will I not heare yow; for your handes are full of blood." But most plainely to our purpose speaketh the same Prophet, saying: "The hous of Jacob daylie seaketh me, and they wolde knowe my wayes, as a nation that wrought justice, and that had not left the judgement of their God. They ask me judgementes of justice (that is, they querrell with me), and they desyre that God shall drowe neare. Why have we fasted (say they) and thou beholdest not? We have afflicted our soules, and thow misknowest it." The Prophet answereth in the persone of God, and sayeth, "Beholde in the day of your Faste, ye will seak your will, and require all your dettes: beholde ye faste to strife and debaite, and to smyte with the fist of wickednes: ye shall not Faste as they do to daye, to make your voice be heard above," that is, to oppresse uthers; so that they are compelled to crye unto God. "Is it suche a Faste that I have chosen? That a man shuld afflict his soule for a day, and to bow downe his head as a bulrash, and to ly downe in sackcloth and ashes? Wilt thow call this a Fasting, or an acceptable day unto the Lord? Is not this the Fasting that I have chosen, to louse the bandes of wickednes, to take of the heavie burdinges, and to let the oppressed go fre, and that ye break everie yock? Is it not to deale thy bread unto the hongrie; and that thow bring the poore that wandreth unto thy hous? When thow seest the nacked, that thow cover him; and hyde not thyself from thy owen fleshe. Then shall thy light break furth as the morning, and thy health shall growe spedelie, thy righteousnese shall go before thee, and the glorie of the Lord shall embrase thee," etc. In these most notable sentences, and in suche as follow in the same place, we have to marck what thinges may make our Fasting to be rejected of God; what he craveth of suche as faste frutfullie; and what promes he maketh to such as obey him. This people externallie professed God, they daylie sought his face, by reparing to the Temple, hear-

ON FASTING.

ing of the Law, and exercising of the sacrifices; yet did God plague them in mo sortes then one, as in the Bookis of the Kinges and Cornickles we may read. In their extremitie they ran (as to them appeared) to the uttermoste refuge, they Fasted, and unfeanedly humbled their bodies, for that the Prophet meaneth, when that he sayeth, that they Fasted till that their neckes were weakned, and made faint as a bullrashe, for verray lacke of corporall foode. They layed of their gorgious garmentes, and put on sackcloth, &c.; and yet wer their troubles nothing releved. And that wes the cause why they querreled with God, and said: "Why have we fasted, and thou hast not sene?" &c. And in verray deed to the natural man it wes strange; for God had promised that he wolde conforte his people whensoever they shuld humble themselves before him, notwithstanding their former iniquitie.

In the externall ceremonies, nor in the corporall exercises, there could no fault be espyed. Why then doeth not God heare them? complaine they? God answereth, that their outwarde profession wes but hypocrisie, their Fasting wes but mocking of God, and their prayers could do nothing but provoke him to further displeasure. Because that albeit they reteaned the Name of God, and albeit that they appeared in his Temple, yet had they forsaken bothe his judgementes, statutes, and holie ordinances. Albeit the bodie stouped, and wes afflicted by fasting, yet remained the heart proude and rebellious against God, for they followed their owen corrupted wayes: they oppressed suche as were subject unto them, their heavie yock lay upone the neckes of suche as could not ridde themselves from their bondage. Amonges them were stryfe, debaite, whisperinges of malice, yea open contention and manifest violence, which all were evident declarations of proud heartes, and impenitent soulles. And therefore God giveth unto them open defyance, in the tyme when they think that they seak his peace moste earnestly. And hereto ought we this day, that professe the Lord Jesus, and have renounced abhominations of Papistrie within the Realme of Scotland, give diligent head. For it is not the semple knoweledge of the trueth onelie, nor yet the externall profession of the same, that is acceptable before God. Nay, nay, deare Brethrene, he requireth the frutes of repentance, and they are, to declyne from evill, and to do good, as we may read in many places of the Scripture. Think we it a thing agreeable with the nature of the Eternall our God, that he shall receave us in favour, after that we have offended, and we will not for his saike remit the injuries that are done to us? Can we thinke to be at peace with him, when that we stubburnelie will continew in strife amonges our selves? Shal he relieve our greif, bondage, or yock, and we will not relieve the burdinges that unjustly we lay upone our brethrene? Shal he bestowe his undeserved mercie upon us, and we can showe no bowels of mercie to such as we se in miserie before our eyes? Let us not be deceaved, God can not deny himself. Murther, malice, hatrent, crueltie, oppression, stryfe, thift, deceat, injust dealing, covetousnes, avaritiousnes, and unmercifulnes unto the poore, besydes pryde, horedome, adulterie, wantonnes, and the rest of the workes of the flesh, are so odious before God, that whill that any of them reigneth in the heart of man, he and his whole workes are detestable before God. And therefore if we desyre that God's fearfull judgementes shalbe stayed, let us (that knowe the trueth, and say that we professe the same) unfenedlie returne unto our God. Let us not be inferioures to the king of Ninivie, who commanded everie man to turne from his wicked wayes, and from the iniquitie that wes in his hands. Let us considder what our God craveth of us; but especiallie let Earles, Lordes, Barrons, burgesses, and artificers, considder by what meanes their substances are increassed.

It is not yneugh to justifie us before God, that Civile Lawes cannot accuse us. Nay, Brethrene, the eyes of our God pearseth deaper then mannes law can streache. The law of man cannot convict the Earle, the Lord, the Barrone, or Gentilman, for oppressing of the poore labourers of the ground; for his defence is ready, I may do with my owen as best pleaseth me. The Merchand is just yneugh in his owen conceat, if before men he can not be convict of thift and deceat. The Artificer and Craftisman thinketh himselfe fre before God, albeit that he nether worke sufficient stuffe, nor yet sell for reasonable price: The worlde is evil (sayeth he), and how can men live if they do not as uther do? And thus doeth every man leane upon the iniquitie of an other, and thinketh himself sufficientlie excused when that he meitteth craft with craft, and repulseth back violence ether with deceat or els with open injurie. Let us be assured, deare brethren, that these be the sinnes which heretofore have provoked God, not onlie to plague, but also to destroy, and utterlie overthrowe stronge realmes and flourishing commonwealthes.

Now, seing that the justice and judgementes of our God abyde for ever, and that he hath solempnedlie pronounced, that everie realme, nation, or cietie that sinneth, as did Juda and Jerusalem, shall be likewise punished. Let that fearefull destruction that came upone them, into the whiche, after honger and pest, the sworde devoured without discretion the ryche and poore, the noble, and those that were of basse degre; the yong and olde, the priests and prophetes, yea, the matrones and virgines, eschaped not the day of that sharp visitation. Let their punishment (we say) provoke us to repentance; and so no dout we shall finde favour in the sight of our God, albeit that he hath begune to shew unto us evident signes of his displeasure justlie conceaved against us. But (as God forbide) if we mocke his Messingers, and despyse his wordes, till that there be no remeadie, as they did, then can we (whome God hath rased up to instruct and forewarne yow) do nothing but take witnesse of

ON FASTING.

heaven and earth, yea, and of your owen conscience, that we have faithfullie instructed yow in the right way of God, aswell concerning his trew worshipping as in doing of your dewties one to another; and also that we have forewarned yow of the plagues to come, firste by our tounges, and now by our pen, for a perpetuall memoriall to the posteritie that shall follow, who shall glorifie God ether for your conversion, or els for your just condemnation and seveire punishmentes, if ye continew inobedient.

To prescrive to everie man his dewtie in particulare, we can not, because we knowe not whereintill everie man, and everie estate particularlie offendeth; but we must remit every estate, and everie man in his vocation to the examination of his owen conscience; and that according as God commandeth in his hole Law, and as Christ Jesus requireth, that suche as shall possesse the kingdome with him shall do: which is, "Whatsoever (sayeth he) that ye wolde men shulde do unto yow, do ye the like unto them." By this reule, whiche the author of all equitie, justice, and policie hath established, send we the Earles, Lordes, Barrons, and gentilmen to trye their owen consciences, whether that they wolde be content that they shuld be entreated (if God had made them husbandmen and laubowrers of the ground), as they have entreated, and presentlie doeth entreate, suche as sometymes had a moderate and resonable life under their predecessours; whether, we say, that they wolde be content that their steadinges and malinges should be raised from male to ferme, from one ferme to two, and so going upward, till that for povertie the ancient laubourers are compelled to leave the ground in the handes of the lord. If with this entreatment they wolde be content, we appeale [to] their owen conscience; and if they thinke that they wolde not, then, in God's Name we require them to begin to reforme themselves, and to remember that it is not we, but that it is Christ Jesus that so craveth of them. And unto the same reule we send Judges, Lawers, Merchandes, Artificers, and finallie, even the verray labourers of the ground themselves, that everie one in his vocation may trye how justlie, uprightlie, and mercyfullie he dealeth with his Nighboure: And if he finde his conscience accused by the former sentence of our Master, let him call for grace, that he may not onelie repent for the by past, but also amend in tymes to cume; and so shall their Fasting and Prayers be acceptable unto God.

If men think that we require the thing that is unpossible, for what were this els but to reforme the face of the whole earth? which never wes, nor yet shalbe, till that the righteous King and Judge appeare for the restauration of all thinges: We answer, that we speak not to the godless multitude, nether yet to such as are mockers of God's judgementes, whose portion is in this life, and for whome the fyre of hell (which now they mock) is assuredlie prepared. But we speak to such as have professed the Lord Jesus with us, who have communicated with his blessed Sacramentes, have renounced idolatrie, and have avowed themselves to be new creatures in Jesus Christ, in whome they are ingrafted as livelie branches, apt to bring furth good frute. Now, why it shuld be thought unpossible that these men (of what vocation that ever they be) shulde begin to expresse in their lives, that which in worde they have publictlie professed, we se no good reasone, unles that we wolde say that it is unpossible that God shall now work in men of this age, as we read that he hath wrought in men before us; and that were blasphemie.

Seing that the hand of our God is no more shortned towardes us then it hath bene towardes those that have passed before us. At God's semple commandement, Abraham left his father's hous and native countrie. Moyses preferred the condition of the people of Israell, even in their greatest affliction, to the ryches and glorie of Pharos Courte. David, upon the unction of Samuell, did pacientlie abide the persecution of Saul many yeares. Zacheus, at an dennar with Christ Jesus, wes not onelie content to restore whatsoever he had before defrauded, but also to give the half of all his substance to the sustentation of the poore. And the faithfull, in the dayes of the Apostles, solde their possessions and ministrat unto the indigent. None of these excellent workes crave we of the faithfull in our age, but onely those without the which the spirite of sanctification cannot be knowen to be in man; to wit,

that everie man speak the trueth with his brother;
that none oppresse nor defraude another in any
busynes; that the bowels of mercy may appeare
amongs suche as God hath called to his knoweledge;
and finally, that we altogether that professe the
Lord Jesus, and do abhorre idolatrye, abhorre also
all kynde of impietie, studying to abound in all
good workes, and to shyne as lyghtes in the
middest of this wicked generation: which, if we
do not, we declare, no dout, that Christ Jesus
dwelleth not within us, but that we ar they
that heare and knowe the will of our Lord, but
do not the same. And unto what curse and
malidiction suche persones are subject, the parable
of the fegge-tre, which wes threatned to be cut
downe if it brought not furth frute; the curse
given to it, upon the which Christ Jesus, being
hongrie, fand no frute, and his last sentence
against the reprobate, do sufficiently witnes. In
the which we have to observe, that the reprobate
are adjudged to the fyre that never shalbe quenched,
not onely because they committed iniquitie, but
also because they were not found frutefull in good
workes. Let everie man, therefore, that will
avoyde plagues temporall and perpetuall, un-
feanedlie studie to accomplishe in worke that
which in worde and outwarde profession he doeth
avowe; and upone suche, no dout, shal the blessing of God rest, when the manifest contempners
and cloked hypocrites shal be rased from the
face of the earth, and shalbe cast unto uttermoste
darkenes, where there shalbe weaping and gnashe-

ing of teith without end, whiche shalbe the rewarde of all their wicked workes.

Mo thinges we wolde have written, suche as the notes upone the disconfiture of Joshua at Hay, and of the Israelites fighting against Benjamin, together with the foolishe opinion of the Papistes, who think themselves oblished to fast fourtie dayes (whiche they call their Lent), because that Christ Jesus fasted fourtie dayes immediatlie after his Baptisme: but these we are compelled for this present to pretermit, be reason that the tyme appoynted to this present exercise of Fasting approcheth so nye. If God of his mercy shall please to continew the light of his Evangle amonges us, this argument will be enlarged and set furth with greater circumstances from tyme to tyme.

The Ordour of the Fast.

Now to the Ordour, Exercise, and Abstinence that is to be kept in this publict Fasting: First, it is to be observed, that the two dayes before expressed, to wit, the last Sonday of Februarie instant, and the first Sonday of Marche immediatly thereafter following, ar not appoynted for any religion of tyme, nether yet that those precised dayes shalbe observed everie yeare following; but because that shortly thereafter, are the Estates of this Realme appoynted to convene in Parliament, Therefore the whole Assemblie thoght those dayes for the present necessitie most meit;

leaving in the libertie of the Churche what tyme they will appoynt to that exercise in all tymes to cum.

The Sondayes are appoynted not of superstition, nether yet to bring in any schysme within the Church, but because that upone the Sonday the people (especiallie that dwell a landwart) may best attend upone Prayer, and the rest of the Exercises that ought to be joyned with publict Fasting.

THE Abstinence is commanded to be from Setterday at eight houres at nyght, till Sonday after the exercise at after noone, that is, after five houres ; and then onely bread and drinck to be used, and that with great sobrietie, that the body craving necessary food, the soule may be provoked earnestly to crave of God that which it moste neadeth ; that is, mercie for our former unthanckfulnes, and the assistance of his Holy Spirite in tymes to cum.

Men that will observe this exercise, may not any of the two dayes use any kynde of gammes, but exercise themselves after the publict Assemblies in previe meditation with their God.

Gorgious apparrell wolde be absteaned fra during the whole tyme of our humiliation, which is, from the one Sonday in the morning, till the nixt Sonday at nyght; albeit that the straitnes of abstinence is to be kept, but the two dayes onely.

We do not binde the conscience of persones

THE GENERAL FAST.

that be unable to beare the extremitie of the Abstinence; and yet do we exhort them to use their libertie (if any they tak) in secret, least that others ather follow their evill exemple, or els judge them to be despysers of so necessarie an exercyse.

The tyme that shalbe spent aswell before none as after, must be left to the wisdome of the discrete Ministers, who best can judge both what the auditore may beare, and what themselves are able to sustene. But because that this exercise is extraordinary, the tyme thereof wolde be somewhat longer then it is used to be in the acustomed Assemblies. And yet we wolde not have it so tedious that it shulde be noysome to the people. And therefore we think that three houres and less, before noune, and two houres at after noune, shalbe sufficient for the whole exercyse publict: The rest to be spent in previe meditation by everie familie aparte.

The Sonday preceading the last Sonday of February, as before is said, shall everie Minister give advertisement to his flocke of such thinges as are to be done the nixt Sonday following, and of the causes of the same, with suche exhortation as God shall put into their mouthes, to make the people to embrase the just commandement of the Churche with more glaide myndes.

In Townes we think expedient that the exercise of the doctrine begine upone the Setterday at after noone, immediatly preceading the first Sonday of Abstinence, that the people may be the better prepared religiously to use the observations of the nixt day: But in Landwart we think good that the doctrine begine the Sonday before. The argument of the Sermon and exhortation to be taken from some proper place of the Prophetes—as of Joel the first, where he sayeth: "Sanctifie a faste, appoynt the assemble," &c. Or of Jonas the thride, where Jonas cryed, "And yet fourtie dayes, and Ninive shalbe distroyed," &c. Or of Jeremie the sevint where that he sayeth, "Heare the worde of the Lord, all Juda, and ye that enter in by these gates," &c. Or of the threttene of Lucas, upone the declaration of them that shewe to our Master the crueltie of Pylate, and upone his answer. Or upone any uther proper place within the Scripture that entreteth of repentance, of publict humiliation, of the causes, and of the frutes of the same.

This ended, as it were for preparation, the beginning shalbe upon Sonday, from the Law of God, because that all that offendeth God's Majestie proceadeth from the transgression thereof; and therefore, after a shorte prayer, that God will please to make his Holy word to fructifie amonges us, this Confession shalbe made.

The Confession that shal goe before the Reading of the Law, and before everie Exercyse.

It is of thy mercy, O Lord, and not of our merites, that it hath pleased thee to showe thy

THE GENERAL FAST.

self unto the worlde ever from the beginning, and unto us now in this last and moste corrupt age: yea, Lord, we further confesse, that nether Law nor Evangle can profite us to salvation, except that thow, of thy meare grace, worke into us abufe all power that is in this oure nature. For albeit thow teache, we shall remaine ignorant; albeit thow threaten, we shal contempne; and albeit thow promes mercy and grace, yet shall we despaire and remaine in infidelitie; onles that thow creat in us new heartes, write thy Law into the same, and seale in us remission of our sinnes, and that sense and feeling of thy Fatherlie mercy, by the power of thy holie Spirite. To the originall world thou spakest by Noha: To Pharao and his people by thy servand Moyses: To all Israell by the fearefull trumpet of thy Law: To the Cietie of Jerusalem by thy owen Wisdome, our Lord Jesus Christ: And to the multitude aswel of Jewes as Gentiles, by the preaching of thy holy Apostles. But who gave obedience? Who trembled, and constantlie feared thy hote displeasure? Who did rightly acknowledge the time of their visitation? And who did embrase and kepe to the end thy fatherly promises? Onely they, O Lord, to whome thy Spirite wes the inwarde teacher, whose heartes thow opened, and from whome thow removed rebellion and infidelitie: the rest were externally called, but obeyed not: they heard aswel mercy offered as threatninges pronounsed, but nether with the one nor with the uther were they affectually moved.

We acknowledge, O Lord, that the same corruption lurcketh in us, that budded furth in them, to their distruction and just condemnation. And therefore we moste humbly beseak thee, O Father of mercies, for Christ Jesus thy Sones sake, that as thow hast caused the lyght of thy worde clearely to shyne amongs us, and as thow hast plainely instructed us, by the external ministerie, in the ryght way of salvation: So it will please thee inwardly to move our dulle heartes, and by the power of thy Holy Spirite, that thow will write and seale into them that holy fear and reverence which thow cravest of thy chosen childrene, and that faithfull obedience to thy holie will, together with the fealing and sense, that our sinnes are fully purged, and frely remitted, by that only one Sacrifice, whiche onely by it self is acceptable unto thee, to wit, the obedience, death, and mediation of thy onely Sone our soverane Lord, onely Pastor, Mediator, and Hie Preast, our Lord Jesus Christ. To whome with thee, and with the holy Ghoste, be all honour and glore, worlde without end. Amen.

> *This Confession ended, the Minister or Reader shall distinctlie read the 27. and 28. of Deuteronomie: which ended, the Minister shall wishe everie man to descend secretly into him self, to examine his owen conscience, whereinto he findeth him selfe giltie before God. The Minister himself, with the people, shall prostrate themselves, and remaine in private*

THE GENERAL FAST.

meditation a reasonable space, as the quarter of an houre, or more. Thereafter shal the Minister exhorte the people to confesse with him their sinnes and offences, as followeth :—

Just and ryghteous art thow, O Lord God, Father everlasting; holy is thy Law, and moste just are thy judgementes, yea, even when thow doest punishe in greatest severitie; we do confesse, as the trueth is, that we have transgressed thy whole law, and have offended thy godly Majestie, in breaking and violating everie precept of the same; and so moste justly may thow poure furth upone us all plagues that are threatned, and that we finde powred furth upon the disobedient at any tyme from the beginning.

And so muche the rather, O Lord, because that so long we have bene called by thy Holie word to unfeaned repentance and newnes of lyfe, and yet have we still remaned in our former rebellion: and therefore if thow wilt enter in judgement with us, we can nether eschape confusion in this lyfe, nor just condempnation in the lyfe to cum. But Lord, thy mercie is without measure, and the treuth of thy promises abydeth for ever. Unworthy are we that thow shuldest looke upon us: but, Lord, thow hast promised that thow wilt show mercy to the moste grievous offenders, whensoever that they repent. And further, thow, by the mouth of thy deare Sone our Lord Jesus Christ, hast promised that thow wilt give thy Holy Spirite to suche as humblie cal unto thee.

In boldnes of the whiche promes, we moste humbly beseak thee, O Father of mercies, that it wold please thy godly Majestie to work in our stubburne heartes an unfeaned dolour for our former offences, with some sense and fealing of thy grace and mercy, together with an earnest desyre of justice and righteousnes, in the which we are bound continually to walk. But because that nether we nor our prayers can stand before thee, be reason of that imperfectione which still remaineth in this oure corrupted nature, we fle to the obedience and perfite justice of Jesus Christ, our onely Mediator, in whome, and by whome, we call not onely for remission of our sinnes, and for assistance of thy Holy Spirite, but also for all things that thy godly wisdome knoweth to be expedient for us, and for thy Church universall. Praying as he hath taught us, saying: OUR FATHER THAT ART, &c.

This ended, the Minister shall read the Text whereuponc he will ground his Sermon.

First, he shal expone the dignitie and equitie of God's Law. Secondly, the plagues and punishmentes that ensew the contempt thereof, together with the blessinges promised to the obedient observers of it. Thridly, he sall teache Christ Jesus to be the end and perfection of the Law, who hath perfitely accomplished that whiche wes impossible to the Law to do. And so shall he exhorte everie man to unfeaned repentance, to

THE GENERAL FAST.

steadfast faith in CHRIST JESUS, and to showe frutes of the same.

The Sermone ended, the commone prayer shalbe used, that is conteaned in the Psalme booke, the 46. page thereof, beginning thus: "God Almyghtie and heavenly Father," &c. Which ended, the 51. Psalme shalbe soung whole; and so with the benediction, the assemblie is to be demitted for that exercise.

At after noune.

Efter invocation of God's name, publictly by the Minister, and secretly by every man for a reasonable space: The Minister may take the argument of his Sermone from the beginning of 119. Psalme, where the diligent reader shall observe the properties and conditions of suche as in whose heartes God writeth his Law. Or if that be thought over hard, then may ye take the text of Johne, " God is lyght, and into him there is no darcknes: if we say we have fellowshipe with him," &c. The prayer is referred unto the Minister. The 6. Psalme shalbe soung.

The benediction and exhortation, to call to mynde wherefore that exercise is used, being ended, the publict Exercise shalbe put to end for that day.

Albeit, that to Landwart the people cannot well convene everie day betwix the two Sondayes, yet in Broughes and Townes we think they ought to convene an houre before none, and an houre and more at after none. The houre before none to be the houre accustomed to the commone prayers; the houre at after noone to be at 3 houres or after.

The Exercise of the whole Weke.

The beginning ever to be with Confession of our sinnes, and imploring of God's graces. Then certane Psalmes, and certane Histories to be distinctly red, exhortation to be conceaved thereupon, and prayers lykewise, as God shall instruct and inspyre the Minister or Reader.

Mononday before none.

Psalm, 2. 3. and 10.
Historie, 2. of the Judges.

After none.

Psalm, the 12. 13. and 17.
Historie, the 6. of the Judges.

Teusday before none.

Psalm, the 25. and 28.
Historie, the 7. of the Judges.

After none.

Psalm, the 36. and 40.
Historie, the 4. of the Judges.

THE GENERAL FAST. 221

Wednesday before none.

Psalm, the 14. and 55.
Historie, the 19. of the Judges.

After none.

Psalm, the 44. and 56.
Historie, the 20. of the Judges.

Thurisday before none.

Psalm, the 49. and 57.
Historie, Esther the 3. and 4.

After none.

Psalm, the 37.
Historie, Esther the 5. 6. and 7.

Fryday before none.

Psalm, the 59. 61. and 64.
Historie, the 2. of Paralip. 20.

After none.

Psalm, the 69.
Historie, the 36. of Isai.

Setterday before none.

Psalm, the 68. and 70.
Historie, the 37. of Isai.

After none.

Psalm, the 74. and 77.
Historie, the 9. and 10. of Esd.

Sonday the last day of this publict exercise, for this tyme, before none shalbe used in all thinges as the former Sonday, except that the 26. of Leviticus may be red for the 28. of Deuteronomie and for the prayer shalbe used that which is to be found in the Psalme book, beginning, "Eternall and everlasting," &c.

Sonday at after none.

Psalm, lxxviii.
Historie, the ix. of Daniel.

The exhortation and prayers ended, for the conclusion shalbe distinctly read the 80. Psal., and so with exhortation to everie man to considder to what end the whole Exercise tendeth, with benediction the assemblie shalbe demitted.

The Exhortations and Prayers of every severall Exercise, we have remitted to be gathered by the discrete Ministers; for tyme preassed us so, that we coulde not frame them in suche ordour as wes convenient, nether yet thought we it so expedient to pen prayers unto men, as to teache them with what heart and affection, and for what causes we shulde pray in this great calamitie, appearing shortlie to overwhelme this whole Realm, unles God of his great mercy abufe mannes expectation finde the remeady. Before whome it is that we have (and presently do) prostrate our selves, for obteaning of those thinges, without

THE GENERAL FAST. 223

whiche the lyght of his Evangle cannot long continew with us. And therefore, yet ones againe, we exhorte, and by the power committed unto us by God, charge all that professe the Lord Jesus, and the sinceritie of his Evangle, within this Realme, that even as they love the quyetnes of their commonwealth, the continuance of Christ Jesus his holy Evangle within the same, and their owen salvation, together with the salvation of their posteritie that unfeanedly they prostrate themselves, before the Throne of God's Majestie, and in bitternes of heart pray with us, saying,

ARYSE, O Lord, and let thyne ennimies be confounded. Let them fle from thy presence that hate thy godly name. Let the grones of thy afflicted enter in before thee; and preserve thow by thy owen power, suche as be appoynted to death. Let not thy ennimies thus triumph to the end: but let them understand that against thee they fight. Preserve the wyne which thy ryght hand hath planted. Oppone thy power to the power of that Romaine Antichrist, and let the glorie of thyne annoynted Jesus Christ our Lord shyne before all nations. So be it.

Hasten, Lord, and tary not.

Certaine Chapters and Partes of the Scriptures

Used be the Ministers of Edinburgh and Halyrudhous, in the tyme of God's visitation by the Pest; in the tyme when in the Court rang all impietie, as murther, huredome, in contempt of God's word, bot especially in the tyme when the Quene wes strikken be God's hand in Jedburgh: Also in the tyme of famine and derth, and uther suche tymes as God gave occasion, and according to the maner of the scurge.

In tyme of Pest.

The 21. of Numeri, the 34. of the secund buke of Samuel, 3. chap. of Ezechiel, the 91. Psalme, with uther suche places proper for the same.

In the tyme when Impietie abounded.

Ezechiell the 3.
The 1. of Zephaniach.
Numeri the 16.
Numeri the 25.
Josua the 7.
1. of Samuel the 4. and 7.
1. of Samuel the 15.
1. of the Kinges the 13.
2. of the Chron. the 26.
Esayas the 3.
Jeremias the 34.
Oseas the 4.
Amos the 6.
Obadiach.
Micheas the 2.

Zacharie the 5.
Ezra the 4.
Nehemiach. 9.

In tyme of Famine.

Esayas the 58.
Haggeus the 1.
Amos the 4.
Amos the 8.
1. of Kinges the 17. and 18.
2. of Kinges the 4.
2. of Kinges 6. 7. and 8.
Zachary the 7.

And uthers such lyke partes of the Scriptures, according as the correction wes laide of God: For even as the Lord our God hes divers and sindrie wandes wherewith he scurgeth the world; bot mercyfullie correcteth his owen children for their profite, so hes he left divers examples in holy Scripture, how his chosen hes used themselves under everie sorte of correction, by him Fatherly laide upon them, as in the chapters before expressed, wes first noted, to steare man to prevent God's Judgements be trew and unfeaned repentance before the plague came.

So these chapters now noted, wes chosen be the Ministers of Edinburgh and Halyrudhous, and uthers godly their about, at such tymes as God did visite them, as is abone expressed. To testifie alswa, that the Kirk of God, nor the faithfull and discreite Ministers are not bound at everie Humiliation to stick scrupulously to the former, as no uther may be chosen, bot as God changeth his wandes, so may our prayers, with the examples of the Sanctes so afflicted, be changed and ordoured. Nether can the wicked justly accuse us, in so doing, of inconstancie : Bot rather ought the chosen to glorifie God, that our publict Fasting and Humiliation is not bound to mannes commandement precyselie, nor to olde customes, as the Papistes use their ceremonies ; but as God vesies us, so in that maner seak we him as he teacheth us and giveth us examples in his moste holy Word, according to his Fatherly correction.

Three Causes of this Publict Fast.

As in these dayes we call unto him for mercy for our unthankfulnes, being so oft and divers tymes delyvered, and yet his benefites so suddeanlie forget ; in that that we se sinne so to abound in all estates, God's fearefull threateninges not feared, bot the pronouncers thereof mocked and disdaned be the most part of the world.

Secundly, the great hounger, famine, and oppression of the pure, although the riche and wealthy that keapes their corne whill the wyld beastes eat it, feil not the famine, whose plague suddenly followes, if hastely they prevent not God's judgements by unfeaned repentance.

Thridly, and cheifly, we humble our selves,

and call upon our God for the confort and
delyverance of oure afflicted brethren in France,
Flanders, and uther partes: For althought the
plague and cruel Decreit of Trent is begune at
Susan, or rather into fylthie Sodome and Pareis,
that boucher-hous of Sathan, be those mane-
sworne and cruell murtherers, yet their mynde
is no les cruelly bent towardes us: For if they
had not pietie to drink their owen bloodes, and
to se the samin ryn in the streites with Manasses,
mekle less will they be moved with compassion
when they shal onely heir crueltie used against
strangers, except God drowne Pharao, chase and
slay Sennaherib, confound and beate doun with
shame Herod, which muste be through the
prayers of the sanctes of God, humbled under
his mightie hand.

Those, and uther manyfolde Causes, as sinne
unpunished in many places, the craftynes of the
worldelinges, with the appearant deceitfulnes of
fals brethren, moveth us this day to stoup under
his mighty hand, which, we cal unto him for his
owen Names sake, we may do without hypocrisie;
then not douting bot that the fruite and profite
thereof shalbe found and sene, as at divers tymes
we have felt, to his owen glorie, and comfort of
his Kirk; to whome be praise, glorie, and honour
for ever. Amen.

A Forme of Prayers

To be used in Private Houses everie Morning and Evening.

Morning Prayer.

ALMIGHTIE God and most merciful Father, we do not present ourselves here before thy Majestie, trusting in our owne merites or worthines, but in thy manifolde mercies, which hast promised to heare our prayers and graunt our requestes, which we shall make to thee in the name of thy beloved Sonne Jesus Christ our Lord, who hath also commanded us to assemble our selves together in his Name, with ful assurance that he wil not onely be among us, but also be our Mediator and Advocate towardes thy Majestie, that we may obteine all things which shal seme expedient to thy blessed wil for our necessities. Therefore we beseche thee, most merciful Father, to turne thy loving countenance towardes us, and impute not unto us our manifolde sinnes and offenses, whereby we justly deserve thy wrath and sharpe punishment; but rather receave us to thy mercie for Jesus Christ's sake, accepting his death and passion as a just recompence for all our offenses, in whom onely thou art pleased, and through whom thou canst not be offended with us.

PRIVATE HOUSES.

And seing that of thy great mercies we have quietlie passed this night, graunt, O heavenlie Father, that we may bestowe this day wholly in thy service, so that all our thoughts, wordes, and dedes may redounde to the glorie of thy Name, and good ensample to all men, who, seeing our good workes, may glorifie thee our heavenly Father. And forasmuche as of thy mere favour and love, thou hast not onely created us to thine owne similitude and likenes, but also hast chosen us to be heires with thy deare Sonne Jesus Christ, of that immortal kingdome which thou preparedst for us before the beginning of the worlde, we beseche thee to increase our faith and knowledge, and to lighten our hearts with thine holie Spirit, that we may in the meane time live in godlie conversation and integritie of life, knowing that idolaters, adulterers, covetous men, contentious persons, drunkardes, gluttons, and suche like, shal not inherit the kingdome of God.

(∴) And because thou hast commanded us to pray one for another, we do not onely make request, O Lord, for our selves and them that thou hast alreadie called to the true understanding of thine heavenlie wil, but for all people and nations of the world, who, as they know by thy wonderful works, that thou art God over all, so they may be instructed by thine holie Spirit to beleve in thee their onlie Saviour and Redeemer. But forasmuche as they cannot beleve except they heare, nor can not heare but by preaching, and none can preache except they be sent, therefore, O Lord, raise up faithful distributers of thy mysteries, who, setting aparte all worldlie respects, may, both in their life and doctrine, onely seke thy glorie. Contrarily confound Satan, Antichrist, with all hirelings and Papists, whom thou hast alreadie cast off into a reprobate sense, that they may not by sectes, schismes, heresies, and errours, disquiet thy litle flocke. And because, O Lord, we be fallen into the latter dayes, and dangerous times, wherein ignorance hath gotten the upper hand, and Satan with his ministers seke by all meanes to quenche the light of thy Gospel, we beseche thee to mainteine thy cause against those ravening wolves, and strengthen all thy servants whom they kepe in prison and bondage. Let not thy long suffering be an occasion either to increase their tyrannie, or to discourage thy children, neither yet let our sinnes and wickednes be an hindrance to thy mercies, but with spede, O Lord, consider the great miseries and afflictions of thy poore Church, which, in sundrie places, by the rage of enemies, is grievouslie tormented; and this we confesse, O Lord, to come most justely for our sinnes, which (notwithstanding thy manifolde benefites, whereby thou doest daily allure us to love thee, and thy sharpe threatnings, whereby we have occasion to feare thee, and spedely to repent) yet continue in our owne wickednes, and fele not our hearts so touched with that displeasure of our sins as we ought to do. Therefore, O Lord, creat in us new hearts, that with fervent mindes we may bewaile our manifolde sinnes, and earnestly repent us for our former wickednes and ungodly behaviour towardes thee; and whereas we can not of our selves purchase thy pardon, yet we humbly beseche thee for Jesus Christs sake, to shewe thy mercies upon us, and receave us againe to thy favour. Grant us, deare Father, these our requestes, and all other things necessarie for us and thy whole Church, according to thy promise in Jesus Christ our Lord; in whose Name we beseche thee, as he hath taught us, saying, Our Father, etc.

A Prayer to be said before Meales.

ALL things depend upon thy providence, O Lord, to receave at thine hands due sustenance in time convenient. Thou givest to them, and they gather it; thou openest thine hand, and they are satisfied with all good things.

O heavenlie Father, which art the fountaine and full treasure of all goodnes, we beseche thee to shewe thy mercies upon us thy children, and sanctifie these giftes which we receave of thy merciful liberalitie, granting us grace to use them soberly and purely, according to thy blessed wil; so that hereby we may acknowledge thee to be the autor and giver of all good things; and, above all, that we may remembre continually to seeke the spiritual foode of thy worde, wherewith our soules may be nourished everlastingly through our Saviour Christ, who is the true bread of life which came downe from heaven, of whome, whosoever eateth, shall live for ever, and reigne with him in glorie, worlde without end. So be it.

A Thanksgiuing after Meales.

LET all nations magnifie the Lord; let all people rejoyce, in praysing and extolling his mercies; for his fatherlie kindnes is plentifully shewed foorth upon us, and the trueth of his promise indureth for ever.

We render thankes unto thee, O Lord God, for the manifolde benefites which we continually receave at thy bountiful hande, not onely for that it hath pleased thee to feed us in this present life, giving unto us all things necessarie for the same, but especially because thou hast of thy free mercies facioned us new into an assured hope of a farre better life the which thou hast declared unto us by thine holie Gospel. Therefore, we humblie beseche thee, O heavenly Father, that thou wilt not suffer our affections to be so intangled or rooted in these earthlie and corruptible things, but that we may alwayes have our mindes directed to thee on high, continually watching for the comming of our Lord and Saviour Christ, what time he shal appeare for our ful redemption. To whome, with thee and the Holie Ghost, be all honour and glorie, for ever and ever. So be it.

Another Thanksgiving before Meate.

ETERNAL and everlasting God, Father of our Lord Jesus Christ, who of thy most singular love which thou bearest to mankinde, hast appointed to his sustenance not onely the frutes of the earth, but also the foules of the ayre and beastes of the earth, and fishes of the sea, and hast commanded thy benefites to be received as from thine handes with thanksgiving, assuring thy children by the mouth of thine Apostle, that to the cleane all things are cleane, as the creatures which be sanctified by the worde and by prayer; graunt unto us so moderately to use these thy giftes present, that the bodies being refreshed, the soules may be more able to procede in all good workes, to the praise of thine holie Name, through Jesus Christ our Lord. So be it. Our Father which art, &c.

Another.

THE eyes of all things do loke up and trust in thee, O Lord. Thou givest them meat in due season; thou openest thine hand and fillest with thy blessings everie living creature. Good Lord, blesse us and the giftes which we receive of thy large liberalitie, through Jesus Christ our Lord. So be it. Our Father, &c.

Another Thanksgiving after Meate.

Glorie, praise, and honor be unto thee, moste merciful and omnipotent Father, who of thine infinite goodnes hast created man to thine owne image and similitude; who also hast fed, and daily feedest of thy moste bountiful hand all living creatures, graunt unto us that as thou hast nourished these our mortall bodies with corporal foode, so thou woldest replenish our soules with the perfect knowledge of the livelie word of thy beloved Sone Jesus, to whom be praise, glorie, and honour, for ever. So be it.

God save the Church universall; God comfort them that be comfortles; Lord, increase our faith. O Lord, for Christ thy Sonnes sake, be merciful to the communewealths, where thy gospel is truly preached, and harbour graunted to the afflicted membres of Christ's bodie, and illuminate, according to thy good pleasure, al nations with the brightnes of thy word. So be it.

Another.

The God of glorie and peace, who hath created, redeemed, and presently fedde us, be blessed for ever. So be it.

The God of all power, who hath called from death that great Pastor of the shepe, our Lord Jesus, comforte and defend the flocke which he hath redemed by the blood of the eternal Testament, increase the number of true preachers,

represse the rage of obstinate tyrants, mitigate
and lighten the hearts of the ignorant, releve the
paines of such as be aflicted, but especially of
those that suffer for the testimonie of his trueth,
and finally confounde Satan by the power of our
Lord Jesus Christ. So be it.

Evening Prayer.

O LORD GOD, Father everlasting and full of pitie,
we acknowledge and confesse that we be not
worthie to lift up our eyes to heaven, much lesse
to present our selves before thy Majestie with
confidence that thou wilt heare our prayers and
graunt our requestes, if we consider our owne
deservings; for our consciences do accuse us, and
our sinnes witnesse against us, and we knowe that
thou art an upright judge, which doest not justifie
the sinners and wicked men, but punishest the
fautes of all such as transgresse thy commandements. Yet, most merciful Father, since it hath
pleased thee to commande us to call on thee in
all our troubles and adversities, promising even
then to help us, when we feele our selves, as it
were, swallowed up of death and desperation, we
utterly renounce all worldlie confidence, and flee
to thy sovereigne bountie as our onlie stay and
refuge, beseching thee not to call to remembrance
our manifolde sinnes and wickednes, whereby we
continually provoke thy wrath and indignation
against us; neither our negligence and unkindnes, which have neither worthely esteemed, nor

in our lives sufficientlie expressed the sweet comfort of thy Gospel reveiled unto us, but rather to accept the obedience and death of thy Sonne Jesus Christ, who, by offerring up his bodie in sacrifice once for all, hath made a sufficient recompense for all our sinnes. Have mercie, therefore, upon us, O Lord, and forgive us our offences; teach us by thine holy Spirit that we may rightly weigh them, and earnestly repent for the same; and so much the rather, O Lord, because that the reprobate, and such as thou hast forsaken, can not praise thee nor call upon thy Name, but the repenting heart, the sorrowful minde, the conscience oppressed, hungring and thirsting for thy grace, shall ever set foorth thy praise and glorie. And albeit we be but wormes and dust, yet thou art our Creator, and we be the worke of thine handes; yea, thou art our Father, and we thy children; thou art our shepherd, and we thy flocke; thou art our Redemer, and we thy people whome thou hast bought; thou art our God, and we thine inheritance. Correct us not, therefore, in thine angre, O Lord, neither according to our desertes punish us, but mercifully chastise us with a fatherlie affection, that all the worlde may know that at what time so ever a sinner doeth repent him of his sinne, from the bottome of his heart, thou wilt put away his wickednes out of thy remembrance, as thou hast promised by thine holie Prophet.

(.) Finally, forasmuche as it hath pleased thee to make the night for man to rest in, as

thou hast ordeined him the day to travel, grant
O deare Father, that we may so take our bodelie
rest, that our soules may continually watche for
the time that our Lord Jesus Christ shal appeare
for our deliverance out of this mortal life, and in
the meane season that we, not overcome by any
fantasies, dreames, or other tentations, may fully
set our minds upon thee, love thee, feare thee,
and rest in thee; furthermore, that our slepe be
not excessive or overmuch after the insatiable
desires of our flesh, but onely sufficient to content our weake nature, that we may be better
disposed to live in all godlie conversation, to the
glorie of thine holie Name and profit of our
brethren. So be it.

A Complaint of the Tyrannie used against the Sainctes of God,

Conteyning a Confession of our Sinnes, and a Prayer for the Deliverance and Preservacion of the Church, and Confusion of the Enemies.

ETERNAL and everlasting God, Father of our Lord
Jesus Christ, who hast commanded us to pray,
and promised to heare us, even when we do call
from the pit of desperation, the miseries of these
our most wicked dayes, compel us to powre foorthe
before thee the complaintes of our wretched hearts
oppressed with sorowe. Our eyes do beholde, and
our eares do heare the calamities and oppression,
which no tongue can expresse, neither yet alas do

our dull hearts rightly consider the same. For the heathen are entred into thine inheritance: they have polluted thy Sanctuarie, prophaned and abolished thy blessed institutions, most cruelly murthered, and dayly do murther thy deare children. Thou hast exalted the arme and force of our enemies, thou hast exposed us to a prey, to ignominie and shame before suche as persecute thy treuth. Their wayes do prosper; they glorie in mischeif, and speake proudly against the honour of thy Name. Thou goest not foorthe as Captaine before our hostes. The edge of our sworde, which sometimes was moste sharpe, is nowe blunt, and doeth returne without victorie in battel.

It appeareth to our enemies, O Lord, that thou hast broken that league which of mercie and goodnes thou hast made with thy Church: For the libertie which they have to kil thy children like shepe, and to shed their blood, no man resisting, doeth so blinde and puffe them with pride, that they ashame not to affirme, that thou regardest not our intreating. Thy long suffring and pacience, maketh them bolde from crueltie to procede to the blasphemie of thy Name. And in the meane season, alas, we do not consider the heavines of our sinnes, which long have deserved at thine hands, not onely these temporal plagues, but also the tormentes prepared for the inobedient. For we knowing thy blessed wil, have not applied our diligence to obey the same, but have folowed, for the moste parte, the vaine conversation of the blinde worlde : and therefore in very justice hast thou visited our unthankfulnes. But, O Lord, if thou shalt observe and kepe in minde for ever the iniquities of thy children, then shal no flesh abide, nor be saved in thy presence. And therefore we, convicted in our owne conscience, that most justly we suffer, as punished by thine hand, do nevertheles call for mercie, according to thy promise. And first we desire to be corrected with the rodde of thy children, by the which we may be broght to a perfect hatred of sinne, and of our selves : and therefore, that it wolde please thee, for Christ Jesus thy Sonnes sake, to shewe to us and thy whole Church universally persecuted, the same favour and grace, that sometymes thou didest, when the chief membres of the same for anguish and feare, were compelled to cry : Why have the nacions raged ? why hath the people made uprores ? and why have princes and kings conjured against thine anointed Christ Jesus ? Then didest thou wonderfully assist and preserve thy smale and dispersed flocke : then didest thou burst up the barres and gates of yron : then didest thou shake the foundations of strong prisones : then didest thou plague the cruel persecuters; and then gavest thou some tranquillitie and rest, after those raging stormes and cruel afflictions.

O Lord, thou remainest one for ever : we have offended, and are unworthie of any deliverance : but worthie art thou to be a true and constant God, and worthie is thy deare Sonne Christ

Jesus, that thou shouldest glorifie his Name, and revenge the blasphemie spoken against the trueth of his Gospel, which is by our adversaries damned, as a doctrine deceiveable and false: yea the blood of thy Sonne is trodden under fete, in that the blood of his membres is shed for witnessing of thy trueth: and therefore, O Lord, behold not the unworthynes of us that call for the redresse of these enormities, neither let our imperfections stoppe thy mercies from us, but beholde the face of thine anointed Christ Jesus, and let the equitie of our cause prevaile in thy presence. Let the blood of thy Saintes which is shed, be openly revenged in the eyes of thy Church, that mortal men may knowe the vanitie of their counsels, and that thy children may have a taste of thine eternal goodnes. And seeing that from that man of sinne, that Romaine Antichrist, the chiefe adversarie to thy deare Sonne, doeth all iniquitie spring, and mischief procede: Let it please thy Fatherlie mercie more and more to reveile his deceit and tyrannie to the worlde: open the eyes of Princes and Magistrates, that clearly they may se how shamefully they have bene and are abused by his deceivable wayes, how by him they are compelled moste cruelly to sheade the blood of thy Saintes, and by violence, refuse thy new and eternal Testament, that they in deepe consideration of the grevous offences may unfainedly lament their horrible defection from Christ Jesus thy Sonne, from hence foorthe studying to promote his glorie in the dominions committed to their charges, that so yet once againe may the glorie of thy Gospel appeare to the worlde. And seing also that the chief strength of that odious beast consisteth in dissension of Princes, let it please thee, O Father, which hast claimed to thy selfe to be called the God of peace, to unite and knit in perfect love, the hearts of al those that loke for the life everlasting. Let no craft of Satan move them to warre one against another, neither yet to mainteine by their force and strength that kingdome of darkenes: but rather that godly they may conspire (illuminated by the word) to roote out from among them, all supersticion, with the mainteiners of the same.

These thy graces, O Lord, we unfainedly desire to be powred foorth upon all realmes and nations, but principally, according to that duetie which thou requirest of us, we moste earnestly require, that the hearts of the inhabitants of England and Scotland, whome the malice and craft of Satan and of his suppostes, of many yeeres have dissevered, may continue in that godlie unitie, which now of late it hath pleased thee to give them, being knit together in the unitie of thy word: open their eyes, that clearly they may beholde the bondage and miserie which is purposed against them both: and give unto them wisdome to avoide the same in suche sort, that in their godly concorde, thy name may be glorified, and thy dispersed flocke comforted and relieved.

The commune welthes, O Lord, where thy

Gospell is truely preached, and harbour graunted to the afflicted members of Christs bodie, we commend to thy protection and mercie: Be thou unto them a defence and buckler: be thou a watchman to their walles, and a perpetual savegarde to their cities, that the craftie assautes of their enemies, repulsed by thy power, thy Gospel may have free passage from one nation to another: and let all Preachers and Ministers of the same have the giftes of thine Holie Sprit, in suche aboundance, as thy godly wisdome shall knowe to be expedient, for the perfect instruction of that flocke which thou hast redemed with the precious blood of thyne onely and welbeloved Sonne Jesus Christ: purge their hearts from all kinde of superstition, from ambition and vaine glorie, by which Satan continually laboreth to stirre up ungodly contention, and let them so consent in the unitie of thy trueth, that neither the estimacion which they have of men, nether the vaine opinions which they have conceived by their writings, prevaile in them against the cleare understanding of thy blessed worde.

And now last, O Lord, we most humbly beseche thee, according to that prayer of thy deare Sonne our Lord Jesus, so to sanctifie and confirme us in thine eternall veritie, that neither the love of life temporal, neither yet the feare of torments and corporal death, cause us to denie the same, when the confession of our Faith shall be required of us: but to assist us with the power of thy Sprite, that not onely boldely we may confesse thee, O Father of mercies, to be the true God alone, and whome thou hast sent, our Lord Jesus to be the only Saviour of the worlde, but also, that constantly we may withstand all doctrine repugning to thine eternal trueth, reveiled to us in thy most blessed word. Remove from our hearts the blinde love of our selves, and so rule thou all the actions of our lyfe, that in us thy godly Name may be glorified, thy Church edified, and Satan finally confounded by the power and meanes of our Lord Jesus Christ, to whome with thee and the Holie Sprit, be all praise and glorie, before thy Congregations now and ever. So be it.

Arise, O Lord, and let thyne enemies be ashamed, let them flee from thy presence that hate thy godly Name; let the grones of thy prisoners entre in before thee, and preserve by thy power suche as be appointed to death: let not thyne enemies thus triumph to the end, but let them understand that against thee they fight. Preserve and defend the Vine which thy right hand hath planted, and let all nations se the glorie of thyne anointed.

Hasten Lord, and tary not.

A Godlie Prayer to be said at all Times.

HONOUR and praise be given to thee, O Lord God Almightie, moste deare Father of heaven, for all thy mercies and loving kyndenes shewed unto us, in that it hath pleased thy gracious goodnes, frely and of thyne owne accorde, to elect and chuse us to salvation before the beginning of the worlde: and even lyke continuall thankes be given to thee for creating us after thyne owne image; for redeming us with the precious blood of thy deare Sonne, when we were utterly lost; for sanctifying us with thyne Holy Spirit in the revelacion and knowledge of thine holy worde; for helping and succouring us in all our neds and necessities; for saving us from all dangers of bodie and soule; for comforting us so fatherly in all our tribulacions and persecutions; for sparing us so long, and giving us so large a tyme of repentance. These benefites, O moste mercyfull Father, lyke as we acknowledge to have received them of thyne onely goodnes, even so we beseche thee, for thy deare Sonne Jesus Christs sake, to graunt us alwayes thyne Holie Sprit, whereby we may continually growe in thankfulnes towardes thee, to be led into all trueth, and comforted in all our adversities. O Lord, strengthen our faith: kindle it more in ferventnes, and love towardes thee, and our neighbours for thy sake. Suffer us not, moste deare Father, to receive thy worde any more in vaine, but grant us alwayes the assistance of thy grace and Holie Sprite, that in heart, worde, and dede, we may sanctifie and do worship to thy Name.

Helpe to amplifie and increase thy Kingdome, that whatsoever thou sendest, we may be heartly wel content with thy good pleasure and will. Let us not lacke the thing, O Father, without the which we can not serve thee: but blesse thou so all the workes of our handes that we may have sufficient, and not to be chargeable, but rather helpfull unto others: be mercifull, O Lord, to our offences. And seing our dette is great, which thou hast forgiven us in Jesus Christ, make us to love thee, and our neighbours so muche the more. Be thou our Father, our Captaine and Defender in all tentations; holde thou us by thy mercyfull hand, that we may be delivered from all inconveniences, and end our lives in the sanctifying and honour of thine holie Name, through Jesus Christ our Lord and onely Saviour. So be it.

Let thy mightie hand and outstretched arme, O Lord, be stil our defence: thy mercie and loving kyndnes in Jesus Christ thy deare Sonne, our salvation: thy true and holie word our instruction: thy grace and Holie Sprite, our comfort and consolation unto the end, and in the end. So be it.

O Lord, increase our faith.

A Prayer to be said of the Childe, before he studie his Lesson.

Out of the 119. Psalme.—Wherein shal the Child addresse his way? in guiding himselfe according to thy worde. Open myne eyes, and I shal knowe the merveiles of thy Law. Give

*me understanding, and I shal kepe thy Law,
yea I shal kepe it with mine whole heart.*

LORD, which art the fountaine of all wisedome and knowledge, seing it hath pleased thee to give me the meane to be taught in my youth, for to learne to guide me godly and honestly all the course of my life; it may also please thee to lighten myne understanding (the which of it selfe is blinde), that it may comprehend and receive that doctrine and learning which shalbe taught me: it may please thee to strengthen my memorie to kepe it well; it may please thee also to dispose myne hearte willinglie to receive it with suche desire as apperteineth, so that by myne ingratitude, the occasion which thou givest me, be not lost. That I may thus do, it may please thee to powre upon me thyne Holie Sprit, the Sprit, I say, of all understanding, trueth, judgement, wisdome, and learning, the which may make me able so to profite, that the paines that shalbe taken in teaching me be not in vaine. And to what studie so ever I apply my selfe, make me, O Lord, to addresse it unto the right end: that is, to knowe thee in our Lord Jesus Christ, that I may have ful trust of salvation in thy grace, and to serve thee uprightly according to thy pleasure, so that whatsoever I learne, it may be unto me as an instrument to help me thereunto.

And seing thou dost promise to give wisdome to the lytle and humble ones, and to confounde the proude in the vanitie of their wits, and lykewise to make thy selfe knowen to them that be of an upright heart, and also to blynde the ungodly and wicked : I beseche thee to facion me unto true humilitie, so that I may be taught first to be obedient unto thee, and next unto my superiors, that thou hast appointed over me: further, that it may please thee to dispose mine heart unfeinedly to seke thee, and to forsake all evil and filthie lustes of the flesh : And that in this sorte, I may now prepare my selfe to serve thee once in that estate which it shal please thee to appoint for me, when I shal come to age.

Out of the 25 Psalme.—The Lord reveileth his secrets unto them that feare him, and maketh them to knowe his alliance.

A Prayer to be said before a Man begin his Worke.

O LORD GOD, moste merciful Father and Saviour, seing it hath pleased thee to command us to travel, that we may relieve our nede, we beseche thee of thy grace so to blesse our labour, that thy blessing may extend unto us, without the which we are not able to continue, and that this great favour may be a witnesse unto us of thy bountifulnes and assistance, so that thereby we may know the fatherlie care that thou hast over us. More over, O Lord, we besech thee, that thou wouldest strengthen us with thine Holy

Sprite, that we may faithfully travel in our state and vocation without fraude or deceit: and that we may indeavour our selves to followe thine holy ordinance, rather then to seke to satisfie our griedie affections or desire to gaine. And if it please thee, O Lord, to prosper our labour, give us a mynde also to help them that have nede, according to that abilitie that thou of thy mercy shalt give us, and knowing that all good things come of thee, graunt that we may humble our selves to our neighbours, and not by any meanes lyfte our selves up above them which have not received so liberal a portion, as of thy mercy thou hast given unto us. And if it please thee to trye and exercise us by greater povertie and nede then our flesh wolde desire, that thou woldest yet, O Lord, graunt us grace to knowe that thou wilt nourish us continually through thy bountiful liberalitie, that we be not so tempted, that we fall into distrust: but that we may paciently waite til thou fill us, not onely with corporal graces and benefites, but chiefly with thine heavenlie and spiritual treasures, to the intent that we may always have more ample occasion to give thee thankes, and so wholy to rest upon thy mercies. Heare us, O Lord of mercie, through Jesus Christ thy Sonne our Lord. Amen.

THE END.

www.ingramcontent.com/pod-product-compliance
Lightning Source LLC
Chambersburg PA
CBHW070732160426
43192CB00009B/1413